USING NARRATIVE INQUIRY AS A RESEARCH METHOD

Using Narrative Inquiry as a Research Method is the ideal introduction to a growing field of study. A full and accessible guide that covers the theory and practical applications of this qualitative method, it provides researchers with a rich framework through which they can investigate the ways people experience the world depicted through their stories. Looking at how this method can effectively be applied in a range of contexts, it demonstrates the value and utility of employing narrative as a research tool in a range of teaching and learning settings.

Connecting with the broader academic debate on the value of narrative as an alternative or addition to quantitative and other qualitative methods and updated to reflect changes in the field, this book

- explores how to use narrative inquiry and gives tested and applied examples;
- builds on theory to consider practical applications;
- explores the narrative cross-boundaries between research and practice; and
- presents a selection of case studies of research on quality in higher education, internationalisation and quality in cross-cultural contexts.

Using Narrative Inquiry as a Research Method provides the ideal grounding for all students and researchers looking to learn more about narrative inquiry or use this method within their research.

Patricie Mertova is a consultant in higher education policy, evaluation, development and quality. She is currently also a visiting fellow at the Institute for Employment Research at Warwick University, UK. She was previously a research fellow in the Department of Education at the University of Oxford, UK. Her research expertise and interest lies in a broad range of education settings: most extensively in higher education, quality and internationalisation but also sociology of education, adult education, educational development in law and linguistics. She has experience in policy review, analysis and evaluation and has a background in the areas of linguistics, translation, cross-cultural communication, foreign languages, literature and cultural studies. She also has experience in administration related to research as well as consultancy.

Leonard Webster has over 25 years' experience in the higher education sector. Most recently, Len has held senior higher education academic, teaching and learning, quality and compliance appointments such as Deputy Vice Chancellor Academic; Pro Vice Chancellor Quality and Compliance in the Australian private higher education sector; Australian Universities Quality Agency Audit Director; Director of Regulation and Review; Senior Higher Education Adviser for the Tertiary Education Quality and Standards Agency (TEQSA); and Teaching and Learning Fellow. Len holds a PhD from Monash University, is a fellow of the Australian College of Educators, has won several awards for his teaching and learning innovations and has published several books, including *Leadership and Management of Quality in Higher Education*.

USING NARRATIVE INQUIRY AS A RESEARCH METHOD

An Introduction to Critical Event Narrative Analysis in Research, Teaching and Professional Practice

2nd edition

Patricie Mertova and Leonard Webster

Routledge
Taylor & Francis Group

LONDON AND NEW YORK

Second edition published 2020
by Routledge
2 Park Square, Milton Park, Abingdon, Oxon, OX14 4RN

and by Routledge
52 Vanderbilt Avenue, New York, NY 10017

Routledge is an imprint of the Taylor & Francis Group, an informa business

First edition published by Routledge 2007

British Library Cataloguing-in-Publication Data
A catalogue record for this book is available from the British Library

Library of Congress Cataloging-in-Publication Data
A catalogue record for this book has been requested

ISBN: 978-1-138-35479-1 (hbk)
ISBN: 978-1-138-35481-4 (pbk)
ISBN: 978-0-429-42453-3 (ebk)

Typeset in Bembo
by Apex CoVantage, LLC

Printed in the United Kingdom
by Henry Ling Limited

CONTENTS

TABLES

FIGURES

PREFACE

We have attempted to outline one research approach using stories of human experience in teaching and learning, research and professional practice. Our own experience of this approach is one of fascination and inquiry, offering manageable and holistic views of human complexity that seemed to have escaped the burrowing and narrowing nature of other research traditions.

Since the first edition of this book published by Routledge in 2007, it appears that interest in narrative inquiry has not diminished. In the early 2000s, we found the literature on narrative inquiry dispersed across disciplines. A decade on, this still continues to be the case to some degree. However, there have been small groups of researchers who have used narrative in higher education research and teaching and have attempted to raise awareness and interest in narrative research, acknowledging that there is a range of narrative inquiry approaches drawing on theories coming out of different disciplines. Trahar and Wai Ming Yu's (2017a) edited book *Using Narrative Inquiry for Educational Research in the Asia Pacific*, published by Routledge, for instance, brought together a group of higher education researchers and practitioners who have used a range of narrative inquiry methods in a variety of settings. Whilst acknowledging the value of narrative inquiry research, a number of the book's contributors underlined the perception of narrative as an 'outsider' among long-established methods within the dominant higher education disciplines and as a quick and easy method to use and not particularly credible (see Trahar and Wai Ming Yu, 2017b; Juntrasook, 2017; Green, 2017). Researching literature on narrative/narrative inquiry a decade on since the publication of the first edition of this book, we have come across more important and noteworthy arguments about why narrative is valuable as a research method; however, we have not found a single source that would comprehensively explain how researchers should use narrative as a research method. We have identified two textbook-style publications: *Understanding Narrative Inquiry: The Crafting and Analysis of Stories as Research* by Jeong-Hee

Kim (2016) and *Narrative Inquiry: A Dynamic Approach* by Daiute (2014). Whilst these two publications give guidance on how to use narrative/narrative inquiry, they appear to target largely beginning researchers, which is valuable; however, they do not necessarily connect with the broader academic debate on the value of narrative as an alternative or addition to quantitative and other qualitative methods. Therefore, we have attempted to provide an explanation of how we have used narrative/stories of experience not only as a research method but also as a method of course, programme or study evaluation. We further describe in detail a particular narrative inquiry method which one of the authors used in two projects investigating growing phenomena within higher education.

It is hoped that this book will assist those who might be considering using narrative/stories of experience in their research. By its very nature, the use of stories in research means that the researcher has a desire to probe the human-centred nature of learning and the associated issues of complexity in a way that is holistic and transcends traditional discipline divides. Given this, we have outlined not only some of the philosophies and underpinnings but also our experience in using a critical events approach to 'see a way through' the expansive amounts of data that can be collected. It requires the researcher to be brave enough to let the critical events arise out of the data and resists the preliminary design of outcomes so firmly entrenched in other research traditions.

Therefore, this book is purposefully written as a starting point for the new researcher and experienced researcher alike. It offers one view of narrative to those undertaking research methods courses. We believe that narrative inquiry is ideally suited to address issues of complexity and human-centredness, which are critical issues facing all researchers and educational developers in a broad range of disciplines. The book is intended to demonstrate the value and utility of employing narrative as a research tool in a wide range of teaching and learning settings and, therefore, includes chapters on background, methodology and case studies to illustrate the application of narrative inquiry as a research method in a range of disciplines.

Along the way there have been a number of people whose support made this book possible, from those involved in postgraduate research supervision through to colleagues within Monash University and elsewhere in the world. We hope that others will find the journey as rewarding as we have.

Patricie Mertova and Leonard Webster
6 June 2019

ACKNOWLEDGEMENTS

We would like to thank Mr Bill Potter, who provided us with invaluable editorial advice and help. We express our thanks to Associate Professor Sue McNamara for an interview she provided us concerning her experiences with narrative inquiry utilised in higher education research and her story of professional experience as an educational developer. We are grateful to Dr Les Henson for his reflection on the use of narrative in his missionary work and subsequently in his postgraduate research projects.

Further, we are grateful to Professor Jan Holzer for his 'critical event' story, which has provided an insight into the developments in the Czech higher education system after 1989.

Finally, we acknowledge the ongoing support and encouragement of our families (Leonard's partner, Anne, and Patricie's husband, Tim Horberry) in all that we undertake.

Patricie Mertova and Leonard Webster

1

INTRODUCTION

Why narrative?

Over the past three decades and more, narrative has gained momentum in two ways – generally, as a term occurring in educational research literature and, more specifically and recently, as a nascent research methodology in its own right with a potential for use across a wide range of disciplines (from philosophy, education, theology and psychology to economics, medicine, biology and environmental science). Narrative inquiry is set in human stories of experience. It provides researchers with a rich framework through which they can investigate the ways humans experience the world depicted through their stories. To paraphrase the French philosopher and existentialist Jean Paul Sartre from his book *Words* (1964),

> People are always tellers of tales.
> They live surrounded by their stories and
> The stories of others; they see everything
> That happens to them through those stories
> And they try to live their lives as
> If they were recounting them.

Narrative is well suited to addressing the complexities and subtleties of human experience in teaching and learning. This chapter proposes that the narrative inquiry research approach, with its ability to focus on critical life events while, at the same time, exploring holistic views, continues to hold valuable potential for researchers in a broad range of learning areas.

Narrative and human experience

Narrative has depicted experience and endeavours of humans from ancient times. Narrative records human experience through the construction and reconstruction of personal stories; it is well suited to addressing issues of complexity and cultural and human centredness because of its capacity to record and retell those events that have had the most influence on us. Such issues play a significant role in many areas of human activity.

People make sense of their lives according to the narratives available to them. Stories are constantly being restructured in the light of new events because they do not exist in a vacuum but are shaped by lifelong personal and community narratives. Narrative allows researchers to present experience holistically in all its complexity and richness. It illustrates the temporal notion of experience, recognising that one's understanding of people and events changes.

According to Carr (1986), narrative is not associated with short-term elementary experiences and actions but pertains to longer-term or larger-scale sequences of actions, experiences and human events. He argues that action, life and historical existence are themselves structured narratively, that the concept of narrative is our way of experiencing, acting and living, both as individuals and as communities, and that narrative is our way of being and dealing with time.

Dyson and Genishi (1994) contend that we all have a basic need for story, for organising our experiences into tales of important happenings. In narratives, our voices echo those of others in the sociocultural world, and we evidence cultural membership both through our ways of crafting stories and through the very content of these stories. Narrative should not be looked upon as separate from real life but as forming meaningful connections to that life:

> Stories help to make sense of, evaluate, and integrate the tensions inherent in experience: the past with the present, the fictional with the 'real', the official with the unofficial, personal with the professional, the canonical with the different and unexpected. Stories help us transform the present and shape the future for our students and ourselves so that it will be richer or better than the past.
>
> *(Dyson and Genishi, 1994, pp. 242–243)*

This notion is also expressed by Bruner (1994), Clandinin and Connelly (2000), Sarbin (1986) and Elbaz (1991):

> [L]ife as led is unseparable from a life as told. . . . [L]ife is not 'how it was' but how it is interpreted and reinterpreted, told and retold.
>
> *(Bruner, 1994; in Dyson and Genishi, 1994, p. 36)*

> Experience happens narratively. . . . Therefore, educational experience should be studied narratively.
>
> *(Clandinin and Connelly, 2000, p. 19)*

> [H]uman beings think, perceive, imagine, and make moral choices according to narrative structures.
>
> *(Sarbin, 1986, p. 8)*

> Story is the very stuff of teaching, the landscape within which we live as teachers and researchers, and within which the work of teachers can be seen as making sense.
>
> *(Elbaz, 1991, p. 3)*

The interconnectedness of narrative and human experience, as indicated in these quotes, means that professional experience cannot be captured just through empirical methods, summarising this experience and issues surrounding it using statistical figures. Realising that such an approach is insufficient and restricting, this book proposes a critical event narrative inquiry method. It highlights its value and warns of its potential pitfalls.

Narrative as an alternative approach to research: contemporary research issues

By proposing narrative inquiry as an alternative research method, we are by no means attempting to dismiss the usefulness of quantitative methods. However, we believe that quantitative methods can, in many instances, be rather ineffective with regard to certain important aspects of subjects or phenomena under study. We find that they frequently tend to overlook complex issues, which are, for instance, considered significant by the participants in the research. This happens because quantitative methods tend not to have the scope to deal with complex human-centred issues. Therefore, we believe that narrative inquiry has a particular value to contribute, as it is well suited to addressing the issues of complexity and cultural and human centredness in research.

Narrative inquiry is set in human stories. According to Bell (2002), narrative inquiry rests on the assumption that we as human beings make sense of random experiences by the imposition of story structures on them. We select those elements of experience to which we will attend, and we pattern those chosen elements in ways that reflect stories available to us. Narrative is not an objective reconstruction of life – it is a rendition of how life is perceived. As such, it is based on the respondent's life experiences and entails chosen parts of their lives.

Narrative inquiry attempts to capture the 'whole story', whereas other methods tend to communicate understandings of studied subjects or phenomena at certain points but frequently omit the important 'intervening' stages. It studies problems as forms of storytelling, involving characters with both personal and social stories. It requires going beyond the use of narrative as rhetorical structure to an analytical examination of the underlying insights and assumptions that the story illustrates. A key contribution of narrative to research resides in the manner in which it frames the study of human experience. The concept of narrative can be refined into a view that research is the construction (Jonassen, 1997) and reconstruction of personal and social stories. Moreover, the narrative can tap the social context or culture in which this construction takes place. Just as a story unfolds the complexities of characters, relationships and settings, so too can complex problems be explored in this way.

Narrative inquiry has gained momentum in practice and research in a growing number of disciplines, partly on account of the constraints of conventional research methods and their incompatibility with the complexities of human actions. However, the move towards the use of the narrative approach has also been influenced by a philosophical change of thought to a more postmodern view, with its interest in the individual and acknowledgement of the influence of experience and culture on the construction of knowledge. Narratives are also sensitive to the issues not revealed by traditional approaches.

> Particular events become important parts of our life because they provide some meaningful information about who we are, and the narrative forms for representing and recounting these events provide a particular structure for understanding and conveying this meaning.
>
> *(Neisser and Fivush, 1994, p. 136)*

Traditional empirical research methods have narrowed the concept of 'validity'. They regard tests and measuring instruments as the best tools for validating research findings, operating within formal systems and focusing on empirical rigour. Narrative research, on the other hand, does not strive to produce any conclusions of certainty but aims for its findings to be 'well grounded' and 'supportable', retaining an emphasis on the linguistic reality of human experience. Narrative research does not claim to represent the exact 'truth' but rather aims for 'verisimilitude' – that the results have the appearance of truth or reality. As Karl Popper proposed, we can at best demonstrate the falsity of statements, not their truth. Thus, the conclusions of narrative research generally stay open ended (Polkinghorne, 1988).

On the issue of validity in research, Polkinghorne (1988) further points out that statistical results are often interpreted as important, without taking into account that they have probably been selected from the chance drawing of sample elements from the population. In narrative research a finding is significant if it is important. Also, in quantitative research, 'reliability' refers to the consistency and stability of the measuring instruments, whereas, in narrative research, attention is directed to the 'trustworthiness' of field notes and transcripts of the interviews.

> Stories derive their convincing power not from verifiability but from verisimilitude: they will be true enough if they *ring true*.
>
> *(Amsterdam and Bruner, 2000, p. 30, emphasis in original)*

Quantitative research is typically looking for outcomes and frequently overlooks the impact of experience, while narrative inquiry allows researchers to get an understanding of that experience.

Philosophies, worldviews and narrative

Before we become immersed in a discussion of the contributions of philosophies to research, there is a fundamentally important assumption about philosophy that should be noted. This assumption is that philosophical tradition changes slowly in comparison with technological advancement. A particular way of understanding or viewing truth and knowledge (which are philosophical phenomena) typically lasts decades and changes slowly, whereas models of teaching and learning, for instance, may change with each decade or generation, or in response to certain technological advances. Standing back and taking a broader philosophical view of research into teaching and learning may reveal approaches to research methodology that are less affected by the coming and going of technological fads, models or theories.

Philosophy offers three major dimensions: epistemology, hermeneutics and worldview. These dimensions provide a means of relating philosophical thought to educational research paradigms. Banathy (1996) described epistemology as dealing with general questions such as 'How do we know whatever we know?' and, perhaps more importantly, 'What is the truth?' With regard to educational research, the key philosophical issue is the relation between 'learning' as a process and 'knowledge' based on the truth, or what is learnt. Within educational research this issue of knowledge and truth might be viewed as the contrasting positions of the scientific understanding of *truth*, as maintained by Merrill (1996), and the various paradigms of human-centred understanding of *truth*, which is holistic and subjective (Reeves, 1996).

Hermeneutics, the art and science of interpretation, expands on the notions of epistemology and truth in providing a broader framework from which we can view the dimensions of truth as they relate to current research issues. Hermeneutics gives us the framework of modernism and postmodernism through which we can interpret 'how we know what we know' based on the epistemological concept of truth. Thus, taking a modernist perspective, Merrill would possibly argue that 'how we know whatever we know' is born of the objective, one ultimate truth. In contrast, within the framework of postmodernism, Reeves would interpret 'how we know whatever we know' in the light of subjective, multiple truths.

The two frameworks of modernism and postmodernism might be characterised as the major forces of philosophical thought that have influenced – and continue to influence – the changes in thinking behind teaching and learning and subsequent research methods. The concepts of truth contained in these philosophies determine the impact of the philosophies on the perception of reality. It is in this perception of reality that educational research paradigms are particularly interested.

Beyond the frameworks of modernism and postmodernism, the overarching perception of reality, which translates these philosophical perspectives into one's view of the world and thus determines the phenomena of knowledge in each case, is described as a worldview.

Worldview, according to Henson (1992), is the perception of reality based on central assumptions, concepts and premises shared by members of a culture or subculture. Worldviews are encompassed in the stories that are told. Stories are one mechanism of revealing those views in the context of educational research. Modernism reflects one worldview, which helps explain the position advocated by traditional empirical research. Similarly, writers such as Reeves (1996), who perhaps adopt a more postmodern position, will put forward their case from their own worldview. The critical factor is that whereas the philosophies of modernism and postmodernism retain a historical identity, worldview is closely aligned with human factors in any time of human activity and experience.

Narrative across disciplines

Over the last three decades and more, interest in narrative as a general component of educational research and, more recently, a method of inquiry has grown significantly among a wide range of disciplines. The original methodological resources were provided by literary studies and sociolinguistics, and, from these resources, a number of narrative inquiry approaches have developed, underpinned by theoretical grounding in these particular disciplines. Thus, it is important to point out that there is no single narrative inquiry method but rather a number of methods grounded in individual disciplines. These individual narrative inquiry approaches are typically combined with other methodological approaches and philosophies which have been influential in that particular field of study. In considering the future applicability of narrative inquiry as a research method, the only disadvantage from a practical point of view is its dispersed and often piecemeal application. It can be argued that there is currently no readily available unifying narrative inquiry methodological approach that would assist researchers attempting to employ a narrative inquiry approach across disciplines. Thus, this book attempts to fill the gap by proposing a critical event narrative inquiry approach which is not tied with a single discipline.

Narrative research and its proponents

Identification of key players and events assists in setting the background to the rise of the popularity of narrative inquiry in contemporary research. It appears that the term *narrative inquiry* was first used by the Canadian researchers Connelly and Clandinin (1990) to describe an already developing approach to teacher education that focused on personal storytelling. Their work claims that what we know in education comes from telling each other stories of educational experience. So narrative inquiry is concerned with analysing and criticising the stories we tell, hear and read in the course of work. It is also concerned with the myths that surround us and are embedded in our social interactions. Often these stories are told informally. Anecdotes, gossip, documents, journal articles, presentations, media and all other texts and artefacts that we use to construct and convey meaning in our daily lives are the instruments of the storytelling process.

In Australia, for instance, a key player in narrative inquiry is Gough (1991, 1994, 1997), a curriculum inquiry and research methodologies researcher and practitioner. Gough sees narrative inquiry as being emancipatory. He argues that the ways we give meaning to ourselves and others and the world at large sometimes happen through stories, of which we are largely unaware or which are taken for granted.

Reflecting critically on the stories that we read, hear, live and tell may help us to understand how we can use them more responsibly and creatively and free ourselves from their constraints. Gough (1997) maintains that narrative theory challenges us to realise how forms of discourse in the natural and human sciences are themselves ordered as narratives. In effect he contends that narrative theory invites us to think of all discourse as taking the form of a story. Gough views the postmodern tool of narrative as being more sensitive to the subtle textures of thought and feeling, which are not readily accessible in more standard forms of research. In explaining narrative, he uses detective fiction as an analogy. In doing this, he exposes the shortcomings of scientific methods in educational research and identifies the need for narrative-based approaches. Gough (1994) argues that some of the ways in which recent transformations of both detective fiction and educational inquiry can be understood are terms of the cultural shifts signified by various notions of modernism and postmodernism. In explaining the analogy, he notes:

> Over the years, detective fiction has both modelled and provided a critique of culturally dominant forms of social inquiry. In teaching research methodology programmes, I have found it generative to invite students to consider undertaking educational research by watching the detectives – to imagine educational inquiries conducted in the manner of fictional detectives with whom they are familiar and relate their investigatory methods to various paradigms and/or traditions of social inquiry.
>
> *(Gough, 1994, p. 1)*

It seems that even a fairly superficial analysis of this kind reveals that educational research may not always keep pace with the development in the methods of fictional depiction that have accompanied cultural changes in the late modern era. Using the detective stories of Sherlock Holmes and the implicit method of inquiry to compare educational research, Gough looks at the criteria of quests for truth:

> While Sherlock Holmes often appears to be emulating procedures stereotypically associated with research in the natural sciences, the relationships that are assumed to hold between facts and the meanings that may be ascribed to them are very different for fictional detectives and natural scientists.
>
> These facts, that natural scientists discover, are usually produced in circumstances designed and more or less controlled by scientists themselves and are thus already the result of many acts of interpretation. Conversely, the facts in which fictional detectives ascribe meaning often results from deliberate acts of deception by guilty parties. But the problem of deception – deliberate or otherwise – is by no means irrelevant to educational research, especially when it comes to interpreting what students and/or teachers say and/or do when they are being observed or interviewed or are responding to questionnaires.

Another way in which the classic fictional detective departs from conventional understandings of scientific rationalism is exemplified by one of Sherlock Holmes's well known dialogues:

'Is there any other point to which you would wish to draw my attention?'
'To the curious incident of the dog in the night-time.'
'The dog did nothing in the night-time.'
'That was the curious incident,' remarked Sherlock Holmes.

Holmes's willingness to apprehend and ascribe meaning to absence – to perceive the absence of a trace as itself a trace – is a disposition that, in retrospect, seems more in keeping with recent critical and postcritical discourse of social inquiry than with nineteenth century conceptions of scientific method.

(Gough, 1994, p. 2)

In terms of the broad analogies that can be constructed between fictional detection and educational inquiry, this is just one of the countless occasions on which a fictional detective's methods are compared with more conventional methods used by the police. The questions that are asked are fundamentally different and assist in establishing multiple perspectives of a world. Each of these questions seems to be lodged in sensitivity to human actions, understandings and events.

As already noted, narrative inquiry as a specific research methodology was preceded by a more general recognition of narrative as a useful component of educational research. Two significant players who need to be considered in establishing the recognition of narrative are Pinar and Grumet, with work done at the University of Rochester, United States, in the early 1970s to refine an autobiographical method of curriculum inquiry or, as Pinar (1975a) termed it, *currere*. (*Currere* is the Latin root of 'curriculum' in its infinitive form to emphasise experience.) Pinar and Grumet drew on existentialism, phenomenology, psychoanalysis and theatre to reveal how their interpretations of our stories of educational experience influence curricular thought and action.

Grumet (1981) provides some of the most compelling reasons for undertaking this form of inquiry by highlighting the inevitable consequences of our own stories and the ways in which our attitudes, choices and values can be invisible to us. Grumet sees autobiography as a way to get a critical perspective on educational experiences that we might otherwise take for granted, so we can see how our personal histories and hopes shape whatever it is we are trying to achieve in education. For Grumet (1976), the relationship of narrative is conspicuous in two ways. First, experiences are reclaimed through a reflective process that begins by allowing the mind to wander and continues by providing rich descriptions in order to situate the narrative. It is only in the freshness and immediacy of our narratives of lived experience that curriculum can be reconceptualised, because the narratives reclaim entire areas of experience. Second, as these narratives are analysed, interests and biases that are often hidden in the normal course of living

stand revealed for inspection. Narratives as texts, as fiction, as records of interviews or experience represent the way in which we have chosen to order and
interpret our experience and are set to reveal the nature and extent of our interests and needs. In this manner educational experience is reordered into a usable
past and present, with the aim of promoting an understanding of that experience
and perhaps providing insights into our judgements and the need for new types
of practices in a changing society.

Narrative also provides a means to investigate the individual's inner experience
of human activity. Pinar (1975b) offers investigation of the nature of the individual's
experience of artefacts, actors and operations of the educational journey or pilgrimage. This has become a knowledge-producing method of inquiry appropriate
for the study of educational experience. In summary, Pinar's (1975c) early charac-
terisation of narrative method involves three steps:

> First to render one's educational experience into words. . . . The second is to
> use one's critical faculties to understand what principles and patterns have
> been operative in one's educational life, hence achieving a more profound
> understanding of one's educational experience, as well as illuminating parts
> of the inner world and deepening one's self-understanding generally. The last
> task is to analyze other's experience to reveal what I call basic educational
> structures or processes that cross biographical lines.
>
> *(Pinar, 1975c, pp. 384–395)*

Graham (1992) argues that Pinar shifted the focus away from a technical, rational
approach, with its concentration on design and objectives, to the nature of inner
experience.

The appeal of narrative method lies largely in its ability to explore and communicate internal and external experience. It also has the capability of crossing
the boundaries between research and practice. More important, perhaps, is its
capability of encompassing factors of time and communication in change, which
may be key features in dealing with complexity and human centredness. The
features of narrative then need to be explored for the potential strengths and
richness they might offer.

Summary

We all have a basic need for story, for organising our experiences into tales of
important happenings. Narrative allows researchers to present experience holistically in all its complexity and richness. Narrative inquiry attempts to capture
the 'whole story', whereas other methods tend to communicate understandings of
studied subjects or phenomena at certain points but frequently omit the important
'intervening' stages. Narrative research aims for its findings to be well grounded and
supportable – it aims for verisimilitude, producing results that have the appearance
of truth or reality.

Modernism and postmodernism might be characterised as the two major forces of philosophical thought that have influenced and continue to influence the changes in thinking behind teaching and learning and subsequent research methods. Modernism is associated with the scientific understanding of truth and knowledge, claiming that there is one ultimate, objective truth; and postmodernism relates to the human-centred, holistic perspective, maintaining that there are subjective, multiple truths.

Narrative crosses boundaries between research and practice. It is well suited to dealing with aspects of time and communication in change, which might be considered key features in dealing with the issues of complexity and human centredness.

2

NARRATIVE IN RESEARCH

This chapter positions narrative as a research method. Narrative studies problems as forms of storytelling involving characters with both personal and social stories. It contributes to research on teaching and learning through its ability to frame the study of human experience. Narrative can tap the social context or culture in which teaching and learning takes place. Just as a story unfolds the complexities of characters, relationships and settings, so can narrative illuminate complex problems in teaching and learning.

Note that, since Connelly and Clandinin's development of the narrative inquiry research method, the meaning of the word *narrative* in the literature bounces between 'story' and shorthand for 'narrative inquiry research method'. This book mainly uses the term *narrative* in the sense of the narrative inquiry research method, but inevitably, just as in the wider literature, both meanings will be found.

This chapter contains many references from the 1980s and 1990s, as this is the period in which most of the key formational literature originates; however, the popularity of narrative inquiry among qualitative-focused researchers has not diminished until current times. There is, for instance, the *Narrative Inquiry* journal focused mainly on the disciplines of psychology and linguistics around topics concerning personal and social identities. Over the past decade, references to narrative inquiry have been added to encyclopaedias of qualitative methods (e.g. Clandinin, 2006; Clandinin and Caine, 2008). Two textbooks focused on narrative inquiry were published (Daiute, 2014; Kim, 2016), and journal issues were dedicated to articles discussing research using narrative inquiry (e.g. *Irish Educational Studies*, 2018, 37 (2); *European Educational Research Journal*, 2013, 12 (3)). A number of articles and books in a range of disciplines, such as nursing (Wang and Geale, 2015), international business studies (Gertsen and Soderberg, 2011), education and cultural contexts (Trahar and Wai Ming Yu, 2017a; Trahar, 2013; Trahar, 2010) and music (e.g. Barrett and Stauffer, 2009), have also been published, further attesting to the undiminishing popularity of the broadly conceived methodological approach. In more recent times, writers in narrative inquiry have reported on how they have used narrative in their own disciplines rather than reflecting on the overarching theory and usefulness of narrative across disciplines. This continued interest in narrative inquiry is one reason for the second edition of this book. There was an 'up-swelling' of investigation into the use of stories as a research method in the 1980s and 1990s, and although some qualitative researchers have continued to use narrative in their research and have argued for the utility of the method, they continue to admit the ongoing lack of acceptance of this research method among a broader higher education research community. Thus, it appears that narrative inquiry will remain a niche research approach with additional disciplinary theoretical underpinning.

An introduction to story-based approaches in research

Narrative inquiry is human centred in that it captures and analyses life stories. In doing this, it documents critical life events in illuminating detail and yet also reveals holistic views, qualities that give stories valuable potential for research. Stories are a reflection of the fact that experience is a matter of growth and that understandings are continually developed, reshaped and retold, often informally. Powerful insights offered by stories have often been ignored, perhaps because of the traditional predominance in research of the modernist-empiricist view. Yet the prominence of stories in our culture surrounds us in every facet of life – much of our learning and understanding is oral based. Most people enjoy a story. Narrative, and the stories it records, offers research a way to highlight those understandings often not revealed by traditional modes of inquiry.

Four questions serve a useful framework in further exploring the background of narrative and its usefulness from a research perspective. The first question is 'Why narrative?' Answering this question leads to the exploration of the history and importance of narrative in the context of educational research. It incorporates the key players and events in the development of narrative approaches in educational inquiry and seeks to establish the vital link between narrative and human experience. The second question is 'What is the prominence of narrative in research?' Answering this question assists in establishing the existence and spread of narrative in research and the thinking behind it. The third question is 'What are the features of narrative in educational research?' This question leads to the exploration of narrative's contribution as an educational research method and its application across a broad range of academic disciplines. Finally, the fourth question – 'Does narrative provide a means to bring to the forefront features of human centredness in research?' – seeks to explore narrative's vital link to real-life situations, a link often neglected by more traditional research methods.

The following four sections provide responses to these four questions and establish the integrity of narrative as a research method. They illustrate the sorts of issues which narrative can address and which cannot be dealt with by other more traditional approaches. They also generate a framework for understanding narrative inquiry methodology in research.

Why narrative?

At this point, a few questions might be asked of the reader:

- What was the last story you heard?
- When did you hear it?
- What do you remember about it?
- What was the last story you told?
- To whom did you tell it?

If memory even half serves us, we could all respond easily to these questions. The prominence of stories in human experience should not surprise us – we come across them all the time. As well as the stories we directly tell or hear, there are those we overhear – on the train, in the bank, in the staffroom. The amount of storytelling that occurs in the many settings that we as human beings come into contact with each day reveals the significance of this most vital aspect of human communication. We rarely get through a day without either hearing or reading a story in whole or in part or telling one to someone else. This condition of being surrounded by stories no matter where we turn encourages us to take them for granted.

However, in the context of research, what makes them noteworthy is their educational value. Unlike many of the stories we encounter elsewhere, those we read and hear in the teaching and learning context are usually intended to help us learn – either directly about the subject matter of instruction or, alternatively, about the strengths or shortcomings of the teaching itself. This fundamental link of narrative with teaching and learning as human activities directly points to its value as an educational research tool. However, the value of narrative is not only restricted to research on teaching and learning – it can be valuable to research in a wide range of other areas, such as medicine, science, economics, politics and law.

McEwan and Egan (1995) note two contributions of narrative to research. First, narrative provides an account of the history of human consciousness. Stories relate the life journey of the human species and the changes that have marked our development as thinking beings. These are stories of knowledge, discovery and exploratory voyages that culminate in our modern conception of science, the arts, human projects and practices. These stories include those by prominent writers and scholars such as Hegel, Plato, Rousseau, Marx and Heidegger, to name but a few. These narratives contain accounts of human progress, perfectibility, decline and loss within a framework of culture and worldview.

Second, at the level of individual consciousness, stories record personal consciousness from infancy through youth and adulthood to old age. McEwan and Egan (1995) maintain that these stories are most frequently represented in literature. These stories make up the wealth of moral tales: autobiographies, confessions, biographies, case studies, fables and any number of other didactic forms. Dewey's philosophy of education, as noted in McEwan and Egan (1995), uses narrative. Dewey associates storytelling or narrative with levels of consciousness and literacy:

> Thus, for example, the forms of consciousness that we identified with oral societies have an important function to play in the growth of literacy in modern society. The later stages of consciousness depend on the earlier ones for their development, not just in the history of the growth of mind but also in the mind of each learner.
>
> *(McEwan and Egan, 1995, p. x)*

Narrative, in Dewey's view, gives us an avenue into human consciousness and thus may be a powerful tool in tapping into the complexities of human centredness in a wide range of environments where learning takes place. As McEwan notes, story is important in oral cultures; to the extent that Western culture retains oral practices, so will narrative have an important and fundamental role in learning (in its broadest sense) within this culture.

Stories continue to form the intellectual and practical nourishment of oral cultures. Other works that have explored the narrative (Britton, 1970; Rosen, 1985; Hardy, 1977; Bruner, 1986; Geertz, 1973; MacIntyre, 1981) support the trend in the recognition of the importance of narrative in learning. They argue that narrative is vital in the learning process in that it constructs the outer environment of communication and action, while simultaneously constructing the inner one of thought and intent. Narrative delves beneath the outward show of behaviour to explore thoughts, feelings and intentions.

If narrative is fundamental to communication, then the use of narrative as a research method may, for instance, give us a better understanding of teaching, learning and performance in a wide range of environments and may assist in generating more appropriate teaching and learning tools and techniques.

Further, narrative has implications for our view of the learner. A concern for the narrative brings to the forefront features of the learner's thinking and learning needs that may have been neglected through more traditional research methods. While the use of narrative as a research paradigm has not been widely accepted until recently, it is now gaining momentum in a number of disciplines and particularly in educational research (Theobald, 1998; Toffler, 1998).

Emerging prominence of narrative in educational research

Angus (1995) argued that narrative is a respectable method for academic writing on teaching and learning, although until recently researchers have avoided it. Angus stated that both fictional and non-fictional narratives on teaching provide a more accessible source of knowledge about teaching than scientific accounts, although they have been held in low repute in the academic community, for the perceived lack of scientific method. Ommundsen (1993) reports that some sociologists of science, in developing their own approaches, argue that true stories about the world, in order to be true, must acknowledge the storytelling process.

Conventional writing practices of much educational research rarely encompass the narrative complexities that may be needed to represent and question educational experience. The storytelling practices reproduced in conventional educational research and teacher education reflect what Harding (1986) called 'the longing for one true story', which has been the psychic motor for Western science. That is, the language of much empirical educational research and literary realism is similar in that descriptions are presented as though they were a selection from a whole, which is the 'real' world. Educational research that embraces storytelling practices is unlikely to tell 'one true story'.

Work by Bruner (1990) illustrates the spread of narrative approaches to educational research. As an influential cognitive psychologist specialising in education, Bruner has reformulated his view of the field, shifting from a more cognitivist view of psychology towards a construction he labelled 'cultural psychology', in which he claims that narrative provides a basis for understanding action. Bruner does not dismiss scientific methods as a means of understanding social phenomena. Rather, he acknowledges them and their important contribution but advances the claims of narrative beyond its traditional basis in literary criticism and literary theory (which is discussed in Chapter 3). Other writers in educational research, such as Gough (1991, 1994, 1997), support this trend towards adopting a narrative approach in educational research.

Gough (1997) argues that the study of narrative is one way of approaching a number of theoretical and practical problems in education. These perspectives are situated in Gough's interrelated worldview and practice as both a researcher and a teacher. He maintains that teacher educators and educational researchers tell stories to learners, colleagues and other researchers.

Educational training is also experiencing demands for different theoretical resources. Placed in the context of reconceptualising the notion of practice in teacher education, Green and Reid note:

> What has emerged for us from this consideration of poststructuralist theory in relation to teacher education, then, is the need and value of rethinking and re-theorising the notion of practice.
>
> This is, and should be quite properly, a significant concern and problem, and in beginning to explore the possibilities provided by poststructuralist theory, we have found a means of attending to, and dealing with the hard questions of pedagogy as complex, contradictory and irrational practices. These are the questions that 'don't quite fit' our usual neat and scientific taxonomies of knowledge.
>
> *(Green and Reid, 1995)*

Viewed in part through post-structuralist theory and philosophy, it becomes clear that the scope for building theory and practice is far too complex to be properly conceived, to be captured or contained within modernist scientific framings or indeed within the discourse of modernism more generally.

The move towards narrative is partly a reaction against the behaviourism of the process-product approach, which ignores instructors' intentions and motives. During the 1980s and 1990s, following the work of scholars such as Shulman (1987) and Elbaz (1991), investigations of teachers' knowledge report anecdotal, narrative evidence (Fullan, 1991). Connelly and Clandinin's (1990) work on teachers' stories, for example, helps promote the legitimacy of narrative in the study of teaching. Ball and Goodson (1985) and others promote an interest in autobiographical accounts of teachers' lives. In addition, there has been a revival of interest in case studies of critical incidents in classroom life authored by teachers. While these studies have been in the realm of teaching, parallels might be drawn with the role of instruction in the fields of adult education and training in the workplace. The role of 'teacher' is synonymous with that of the 'instructor' in these contexts.

Another perspective on the use of narrative can be seen in the writing of research dissertations. Theses in which the researcher has used personal writing to present personal reactions and experiences to the study have been accepted as legitimate grounds for the awarding of various degrees, including masters and doctoral-level awards in education (Hanrahan and Cooper, 1995). Included in the reporting is the reflective process of analysing the research process itself – in other words, exploring the dimensions of narrative inquiry. In the overall process of writing, the narrative is also seen as an iterative process, one of change over time. The research as a whole is conceived as the development of a narrative (Connelly and Clandinin, 1990). It is a jointly developed narrative, with many participants, but told by one narrator who takes responsibility for, and at the same time critiques, the view of intersubjective reality presented at each stage and as a whole.

Hanrahan and Cooper (1995) also note narrative inquiry's embracing of change, even including radical change, during the research process. This allows the researcher to maintain integrity in conducting and reporting the research, because it removes the pressure to present only one single consistent story. Hanrahan and Cooper point out the following about narrative inquiry:

> It freed me from the traditional constraint of reporting the research as though it all belonged within a single paradigmatic structure, and was reported by a single voice. A narrative inquiry research design could incorporate change as an integral and even necessary part of the process of constructing knowledge. It also seemed to me to represent a truer model of how most complex knowledge is constructed than the neater, theory-practice-conclusions, linear model suggests.
>
> Narrative inquiry appears to be able to offer the chance to bridge the divide between researchers and practitioners by allowing practitioners a voice in the construction of new knowledge in the form of the jointly constructed narrative.

> That narrative inquiry has the potential to result in such a narrative which provides a more accessible and compelling record of the shared research to other practitioners than a purely discursive account, is a further advantage.
>
> *(Hanrahan and Cooper, 1995)*

These authors agree with Connelly and Clandinin, who maintain that

> the principal attraction of narrative as method is its capacity to render life experiences, both personal and social, in relevant and meaningful ways.
>
> *(Connelly and Clandinin, 1990, p. 10)*

Interest in narrative inquiry has penetrated both educational practice and research. The prominence of narrative arises in part because of the constraints of conventional research methods and their incompatibility with the complexities of human learning. Moves towards the adoption of the narrative approach have also been a product of a philosophical change of thought to a more postmodern view, with its interest in the individual and acknowledgement of the influence of experience and culture on the construction of knowledge. Finally, it is also important to point out narrative's association with human activity and its sensitivity to those issues not revealed by traditional approaches.

Features of narrative as a research method

The feature common to all stories, which gives them their aptitude for illuminating real-life situations, is their narrative structure. It is not the mere material connection of happenings to one individual but the connected unfolding that we call plot which is important. Plot can be identified as a connection among elements, which is neither one of logical consequence nor one of mere succession. The connection seems rather designed to move our understanding of a situation forward by developing or unfolding it. Narrative, then, is not required to be explanatory in the sense in which a scientific theory must show necessary connections among appearances. What can be demanded of a narrative is to display in what way occurrences represent actions.

The association with action is vital in the learning environment. It is through a better understanding of actions and their demands that the human factors previously ignored are brought to the forefront. These factors then can be integrated, for instance, into the design of training devices (e.g. high-performance aviation and medical simulations training).

Stories allow us to watch what an experience can do to people who are living that experience. It is the precise role of narrative to offer us a way of experiencing those effects without experimenting with our own lives as well. Narrative can allow us to take the measure of schemes intended for human improvement and examine them as a story of experience. This subtle connection with construction of knowledge through experience allows narrative to be associated as a tool of research in conjunction with contemporary learning theories.

Stories contain knowledge that is readily put to use in the world. In many instances, stories do not simply contain knowledge; they are themselves the knowledge we want learners to possess. To be a participant in culture, Kuhns (1974) asserts, is to have experience of the community, the experience of which is expressed through the individual's narrative. Thus, our sense of being part of a community is established, at least in part, by our shared knowledge of a set of well-known stories.

The place of the story and its integrity as a research data source, however, are not without their controversies. Issues of epistemology need to be addressed. One criticism levelled at narrative is that of its subjectivity. Thus, questions about which stories should be incorporated and which should be disregarded pose one type of uncertainty. A second concern is that studies might become trapped into what Connelly and Clandinin (1990) call the 'Hollywood effect', whereby the narrative is distorted to provide a 'happy ending'; that is, it all works out well in the end.

In taking a narrative approach, there are also other warnings to heed. Just as narrative is seductive in its contribution to understanding, so is there an opportunity for misuse. This aspect is argued strongly by theorists pointing to concealed or distorted messages and perspectives in text. In addressing the controversies, Hauerwas and Burren (1989) argue that practical wisdom (i.e. narrative) cannot claim to be a science, because it must deal with particular courses of action (rather than empirically reproducible data). Therefore, subjectivity treated with appropriate care and respect is acceptable and does not belittle the integrity of the approach.

Human centredness and complexity in research

Perhaps the most important features of narrative are those relating to human centredness. These features illuminate the real-life experiences of learners and at the same time are sensitive to the broader connections to the individual's worldview. Narrative's human-centred approach permeates the issues of research measures, action, practice, transfer of knowledge and human consciousness.

Polkinghorne (1988) argues that the validity of narrative is more closely associated with meaningful analysis than with consequences. He also maintains that reliability is not the stability of the measurement but rather the trustworthiness of the notes or transcripts. According to Polkinghorne, we need to reorientate our measures in using narrative. It is not satisfactory to apply the previous criteria of more traditional approaches – that is to say the measures of validity and reliability – to narrative. However, Huberman (1995) asserts that what is sought are new measures such as access, honesty, verisimilitude, authenticity, familiarity, transferability and economy.

Narrative illuminates human actions and complexities. People usually encode their experiences in some form of narrative, particularly in those experiences dealing with other people. Schon's (1983) studies reveal that in the professions that involve working with people, stories and experiences were used to explain and justify thinking and actions. Narration of practical experience comes naturally to most individuals. It is used to recount experience and problem solving. Gudmundsdottir (1995) suggests that narrative is the tool of the practitioners to make sense of experience and organise it into a body of practical knowledge.

Narrative situates itself in practice; that is to say, it is learner centred. Past research approaches to understanding the concept of practice have tended to follow a natural science model. This model separates theorising and practice and risks misconception of the interrelationship between human action and practice by imposing external explanation and interpretation on the learner. Carr (1986) refers to Aristotle's concept of practice, in which human action requires 'its own terms' of explanation and interpretation. These trends cannot be reduced to those of physical explanation. Thus, the reconceptualising of practice may have its most profound impact in high-technology environments, such as air traffic control.

Carr (1986) draws the following conclusion on notions of narrative and practice:

> We encounter practices in the present, at a point of intersection of past and future, but we must understand them as part of a process of change. . . . [T]he business of understanding practices will require us to tell stories about how they evolved and with what purpose.
>
> Practices require, for their full characterisation, descriptions of current actions and language use placed in the context of historical accounts that help to explain how the practices have taken their current shape. . . .
>
> Despite the antiquity of the human practice of making and telling stories, the word narrative . . . [is] quite recent. . . . [It] refer[s] to an open category of discourses that are, in general, involved with the construction and reconstruction of events, including human conscious states, in an order that places them or configures them in such a way that they imply a certain directedness or orientation to some goal.
>
> *(quoted in McEwan and Egan, 1995, p. 179)*

Speech is often structured in this way and so are our practices. The language of practice aims to clarify the purposes of practice. This relationship suggests that we should become more aware of our practice as well as see changes in practices as part of this understanding.

Narrative is a tool for transfer of knowledge. It helps us to understand and to communicate new ideas. Strangely, in those disciplines that have historically been embedded in a scientific tradition are some that have very rich narrative traditions. Nowhere else is this case more apparent than in aviation, where 'hangar tales' (Beaty, 1995; Markham, 1994; Gann, 1961; and others) record stories of experience and provide informal training for aircrew.

Gudmundsdottir (1995) observes that narratives allow us to discover new meanings by assimilating experiences into a narrative schema. Connectedness of the story as it moves through time is seen as the transfer of knowledge, progressing from an incomplete story to a more complete one.

Another significant aspect of narrative inquiry is the issue of complexity, which is closely interconnected with the issue of human centredness. Narratives provide an organisational framework for viewing complexity. Using narrative, it is possible not only to look at human factors but also to consider human factors within a range of learning theories. Narrative reveals the need for different strategies at different times in the story of learning. For instance, the types of strategies required at the initial skill practice stage are different from those required at the deeper learning and expert stages (in the move from novice to expert). Narrative acknowledges that time is critical in the learning process, that deeper learning and expert strategies take a long time to develop and cannot be condensed without risk of simplification or reduction. Further, as complexity increases, research approaches that encompass multiple learning theories are required.

Operationalising the narrative in research

The narrative inquiry method applies the techniques of description – scene, plot, character and events – in drawing the narrative sketches or critical events that constitute the narrative (Connelly and Clandinin, 1990).

Narrative inquiry is interested in exploring complexity from a human-centred perspective – the perspective of students, teachers, instructors, patients, employees or others involved in such a study. Data-gathering techniques which inform the narrative sketches or critical events may include surveys, observations, interviews, documentation and conversations that can enhance the time, scene and plot structures of the critical events. A narrative framework then provides a means of organising the plethora of data gathered through these techniques.

The findings of such studies are presented through the narrative in the forms of scene, plot, character and event sketches related to critical events. It is the relation of narrative to the critical events that makes it a powerful research tool.

Narrative inquiry and mixed qualitative and quantitative research methods

Until relatively recently, quantitative and qualitative methods have been regarded as dichotomous or even incompatible. However, lately, a growing number of researchers have perceived the value of combining qualitative and quantitative research methods. Elliot (2005) documents this, referring to, among others, Laub and Sampson (1998), Farran (1990), Thompson (2004), Pearce (2002), all of whom have combined quantitative and qualitative research techniques in their studies and appreciated it as a worthwhile approach.

Elliot (2005) points out that there is a growing realisation among quantitative researchers that they cannot rely solely on statistical methods but need to take account of other aspects, such as human agency (people's motives and values), cultural influences and the temporal dimensions of events. Thus she proposes research that employs both qualitative and quantitative methods, which can potentially 'capitalise on the strengths of each approach' (Elliot, 2005, pp. 171–172). She argues

> [t]he quantitative methods have proved useful in establishing robust relationships between variables that are generalisable to a population beyond the sample in the research itself, while the qualitative methods have provided evidence about the possible mechanisms that lie behind the relationships detected using quantitative research. Where these mechanisms rely on individual motivations and perceptions, qualitative research can be particularly useful in understanding what lies behind people's choices and behaviour and the meaning they attribute to their experiences.
>
> *(Elliot, 2005, p. 184)*

In capitalising on the 'strong' features of qualitative and quantitative methods, she perceives narrative as forming a particularly valuable 'reflective' link between the two methods. In order to move research issues forward, she suggests that

> it is important to learn to tolerate the tensions and ambiguities that they [i.e. qualitative and quantitative methods] create in our research narratives. These tensions might indeed be productive if they begin to challenge and disrupt the hegemony that currently preserves the dichotomy of qualitative and quantitative methodologies.
>
> *(Elliot, 2005, p. 187)*

The authors of this book agree with Elliot in that there is a real value in combining qualitative and quantitative methods: quantitative methods are valuable in producing aggregate data of large samples, while the proposed narrative inquiry method (as a qualitative method) is better able to deal with issues that quantitative methods are generally incapable of representing, such as complexity and human and cultural centredness. However, it must be noted that the narrative inquiry method, as proposed later in this book, has different assumptions, not only from quantitative research methods but also from many qualitative methods. This becomes particularly apparent with regard to the concepts of validity and reliability in quantitative and qualitative research.

Summary

Narrative inquiry is gradually becoming a respectable method, particularly in educational research, despite being rather niche. However, there is a growing realisation of the significance of narrative as a research method in a wide range of other disciplines that have traditionally employed empirical methods, such as medicine, the sciences, economics, sociology, politics and others. This is hardly surprising, particularly when considering the prominence of stories in human lives in general.

What makes narrative particularly appealing to research (compared with other more traditional research methods) is its capacity to deal with the issues of human centredness and complexity in a holistic and sensitive manner. Further, there is also a potential in combining narrative inquiry with quantitative research methods drawing on the strengths of both types of methodological approaches.

3

PHILOSOPHIES AND THEORIES UNDERPINNING NARRATIVE

This chapter traces the philosophical and theoretical underpinnings of narrative. It looks at the origins of narrative inquiry from early analyses of folklore and fables to contemporary research applications in the postmodern era, such as the structuralist-hermeneutic-interpretivist-qualitative paradigms that may require more holistic research approaches.

Models and theories underpinning narrative inquiry

Stories are one of the first forms of learning that a child encounters in life. Throughout our life, stories shape and characterise the ways in which we interact with people and society and how we process information. Stories are the 'substance' of generations, history and culture. They reflect our journey through life. They may also prove to be an important research tool.

In spite of the fact that stories have depicted experience and endeavours of humans from ancient times, they came to the fore of theoretical analyses only in the twentieth century. The theoretical study of narrative (i.e. stories) originates in the field of literary theory. Throughout the twentieth century, there have been a number of schools of literary and linguistic theory in which narrative has been a major focus. However, the most influential of them were the Russian formalists (e.g. Skhlovskij, Propp, Tomasevskij and Eichenbaum) in the 1920s, followed by the French structuralists (e.g. Todorov, Barthes, Bremond and Genette) in the 1960s. At that time the theory of narrative, otherwise termed 'narratology', was becoming 'fashionable' and was acknowledged as one of the standard disciplines of literary theory.

Within classical narratology, there have been three main perspectives of study:

- *Narrative grammar* focuses on the narrated or the story; its proponents included Propp, Bremond, Levi-Strauss, Todorov and Barthes.

- *Poetics* addresses the relations between the narrated and the narrative, or the story and the discourse; this approach was led by Genette.
- *Rhetorical analysis* deals with how linguistic mediation of a story determines its meaning and effect; this approach was given impetus by Jakobson.

The use of narrative inquiry has gradually gained momentum in recent decades. The 'narrative turn', as it is sometimes referred to, was given an impulse by and has drawn particularly from the French structuralist theories of the 1960s. Barthes, for instance, argues explicitly for an interdisciplinary approach to the analysis of stories, noting that narratives can be presented in a range of formats and genres, supporting a variety of cognitive and communicative activities.

In 1983, in her study *Narrative Fiction: Contemporary Poetics*, Rimmon-Kenan expressed a view that deconstruction, as a then relatively new development in the field of literary theory, enriches narrative theory. Since the early 1980s, narratology has become more enriched by adopting a wide range of theoretical perspectives – including feminist, Bakhtinian, deconstructive, psychoanalytical, film-theoretical, historicist and psycholinguistic. Herman (1999) notes that, since Rimmon-Kenan's publication, narrative theory has undergone a metamorphosis. He suggests that, since the early 1980s, the structuralist theorising of narratology has evolved into narratologies, a plurality of models of narrative analyses. So, particularly throughout the 1980s, narratology has moved from the classical structuralist phase to a post-structuralist phase, characterised by a plethora of new methodologies and research hypotheses.

Narratology was originally driven by an ambition to raise literary studies to the degree of scientific rigour and technical precision that was supposed to be achieved by structural linguistics. Narratology as such was invented in 1969 by Tzvetan Todorov in his analysis of Boccaccio's *Decameron*. Narratology was profoundly influenced by French structuralism (structural linguistics), and it focused not only on what narratively organised sign systems meant but also on what they meant as narratives.

From the early 1980s, the narrative approach started becoming popular in a range of disciplines. Some introductions come from the field of literary criticism, where narrative work originated, for example Mitchell (1981). Historians made it clear that stories have an inherently temporal thread, in that current events are understood as rising from past happenings and pointing to future outcomes, for example Carr (1986), White (1981). In psychology, Polkinghorne (1988) explores stories in relation to human sciences; Riessman (1993) offers some introductory methodology; Lieblich *et al.* (1998) draw on individual case studies to demonstrate the ways in which stories can be deconstructed; and Josselson (1996) provides a review of ethical issues in the use of stories in therapeutic fields, with some implications for education. Other significant figures taking the 'narrative turn' include Bruner (1986, 1987, 1990, 2002), Amsterdam (Amsterdam and Bruner, 2000) and Sarbin (1986). In the field of education, the work has focused mainly on teacher education, looking at the ways in which teachers' narratives shape and inform their practice. Schon (1983) emphasises reflective practice; Bell (1997) and Jalongo and Isenberg (1995) focus on listening to teachers' voices and hearing their stories. Connelly and Clandinin (1987, 1988, 1990; Clandinin and Connelly, 2000) have generally led the way in adapting narrative inquiry for educational purposes. Their work offers an introduction to the field for teachers and teacher educators. In the field of language education, the tradition of providing narrative accounts of patterns of language use is fairly well established, for example Heath (1983) with ethnographies and Davidson (1993) with learner biographies.

Another field in which life stories have a significant tradition is sociology. In the 1920s, there was significant enthusiasm about life stories in the context of sociological research. The 'movement' was started in 1921 by Znaniecki, who began organising the first collection of life stories/autobiographies of workers from the Polish town of Poznan. However, Znaniecki's initiative was transformed into a national and recurrent cultural phenomenon only by his disciple, Chalasinski, who showed in his books how the formation and transformation of whole social classes (peasants and workers) could be described and understood by analysing sets of their autobiographies. Life story as a standard sociological tool is also associated with the Chicago sociologists of the 1920s and 1930s. However, they mainly focused on social processes around deviancy (e.g. juvenile delinquency, crime and drug addiction). During the 1940s, the American sociologists entirely abandoned the technique. It was widely and continuously used only in Poland; because of the linguistic barrier, it remained largely unknown outside Poland. Angell (1945) brought together 22 such life story studies, the most influential of which were Thomas and Znaniecki (1958), Thomas (1923), Shaw (1930, 1931) and Shaw *et al.* (1938). Critical essays assessing the method include Dollard (1935), Becker (1966), Angell (1945) and Denzin (1970).

In the late 1970s and early 1980s, all over Europe life stories were written from interviews with old people, but these were written mainly by journalists. One significant sociological work which has highlighted the value of life stories as sociological research tools is Bertaux's (1981) edited collection of studies by academics employing life stories in a range of social science fields.

Philosophies underpinning educational research

Modernism and postmodernism have been noted as significant movements in architecture, the fine arts and literature. However, they have also been influential in other areas, such as social sciences. According to Hlynka and Belland (1991), modernism is aligned with reaction to the earlier twentieth-century machine age. Postmodernism is associated with the age of computers and electronic information design. Hlynka argues that the literature of postmodernism reflects a major concern with the influence of technology on society and culture.

The change in thinking between modernism and postmodernism is commonly called a 'sea change'. This image provides the analogy of the ever-changing sea, in which oceans and currents constantly meet, intertwine and move apart. There is neither a definitive beginning nor an end in this image. Similarly, there is no finite division between the frameworks of modernism and postmodernism. Rather, there is a constant, yet dynamic, motion between the two. In terms of educational research and practice, the analogy of sea change might be likened to the iterative processes that continue to inform and modify our views of the research approaches and consequent practices.

Modernism has its philosophical origins at the time of the Reformation around the 1600s. Modernism draws its origins from the work of philosophers such as Descartes, the seventeenth-century Roman Catholic philosopher, who was seeking a tool to define truth and knowledge in terms of a belief in God and Christianity. He, in turn, was working from the Roman tradition to convince non-believers in times of great religious change. Descartes' premise 'I think therefore I am' is held to be the foundation of the objective scientific tradition. Therefore, truth and knowledge took on a scientific, proof-based logical form. Ironically, Descartes was in essence simply searching for a common ground with which to continue a dialogue with those who did not share his belief. He neither was committed to – nor believed outright in – this definition of truth and knowledge.

Carson (1996) points out that the methods derived from this philosophical perspective were claimed to be transcultural, transracial and trans-linguistic. Put simply, any knowledge produced by these methods was held to be true for all cultures, all races and all languages. The same may be said of the traditional scientific approach put forward by theorists such as Merrill. This objective truth was particularly suited to the sciences.

With regard to educational research, the influence of modernism can be seen in the notions of objective, behaviourist approaches and narrowly defined component outcomes. The contribution of modernism to educational research has its value in simple learning environments and learning systems. However, more contemporary, complex high-performance learning environments and systems would seem to require a more comprehensive and divergent philosophical underpinning as put forward by postmodernism.

Postmodernism, as a more recent philosophical position, maintains that each person brings his or her own 'baggage', or past life experiences, to a situation. Truth and knowledge from the postmodern perspective is a constructed reality (worldview), and there is no objective truth (Carson, 1996). Postmodernism differs fundamentally from modernism in its approach to defining truth and knowledge. Postmodernism rejects the notion that truth and knowledge are to be found through rational thought or method. Whereas modernism values the external, postmodernism values the internal, or the 'I', and puts greater emphasis on human-centred approaches. It therefore has an inherent interest in human factors relating to the acquisition of knowledge.

Postmodernism is also proving to be much more accommodating to the complexities of learning than its predecessor. Given postmodernism's domain of interest in human factors and the acquisition of knowledge, or what might be called learning, it would seem a more appropriate philosophical position from which to launch research, for instance, into complex high-performance learning environments and systems.

Even within the domain of science, with its modernist, objective viewpoint, science philosophers as far back as Polanyi (1964) insist that human knowledge is personal knowledge or personal knowing and that scientific knowledge is not purely objective and exhaustibly verifiable. Moreover, as Carson (1996) claims, once out of the scientific discipline, which is based on modernism, most scientists are postmodern in view. Thus, it appears that there is a natural wave movement or sea change between philosophical positions, which is again determined by context, within the realm of worldview. A closer examination of the natural flow between modernism and postmodernism as they embrace culture is warranted.

Postmodernism, worldview, narrative and culture

From a pragmatic point of view, modernism has made a great contribution to educational research but has not always been extremely sensitive to the various dimensions of learning. Educational research is now beginning to recognise certain strengths of postmodernism. For instance, we are now intrinsically more aware of the diversity of worldviews to a significant degree, because the world is becoming more of a global village.

Worldview, according to Henson (1992), encompasses the assumptions, concepts and premises of a culture and subculture. Kraft (1979) outlines six major functions of worldview:

- It explains how and why things became the way they are, and how and why they continue or change.
- It is used to order, judge and validate.
- It provides psychological reinforcement for the group.
- The worldview of a culture or subculture integrates various elements of the culture.
- A group's worldview functions with some flexibility.
- It enables a people to sort out, arrange and make different commitments, allegiances or loyalties to things that are assumed, valued and done.

Diverse worldviews enable the same event to be looked at, reported and interpreted differently around the world, as the following story illustrates:

> My wife and I had been living among the Momina people of Sumo for only a few short weeks when the red amarilloflowers that I had planted on an earlier visit began to bloom. These beautiful red flowers became the centre of a discussion between Sakee-enee, an old Momina shaman (elder), and myself. 'When are you going to eat them?' asked Sakee-enee with a gleam in his eye, hoping I would share them with him. 'You don't eat these plants,' I replied in my broken Momina. 'They are for viewing, not eating.' Sakee-enee raised

his eyebrows in an affirmative but sceptical response. He left, mumbling to himself.

Similar conversations took place on five or six different occasions over the next few weeks. Each time they ended with Sakee-enee walking away in disbelief. The matter came to a head one morning when, on walking, I discovered my beautiful blossoms had been cut off. Sakee-enee had decided to take matters into his own hands, and try this delicacy for himself. The real issue was that we saw those flowers from different worldviews. His worldview said, 'You plant plants in order to eat them.' My worldview said, 'You plant flowers for their beauty!'

(Henson, 1992, p. 1)

This illustration is indicative of the value of contextualisation and cultural influence on our way of understanding. Postmodernism, with its multiple truths and focus on subjectivity in worldview, seems more capable of addressing educational research needs that incorporate culture than the more objective, reductionist scientific philosophy of modernism. Yeaman (1996) argues that a postmodern approach to educational research has different interests from a modernist approach. Postmodern interests include 'who is doing what to whom' (character, plot and time); multiple voices (truths); holistic views; relationships between disciplines; practical concerns; personal voices; and social, ethical and cultural responsibilities.

Narrative inquiry in the current era

The recent increase in the use of narrative inquiry across disciplines stems from the realisation that the traditional empirical research methods cannot sufficiently address issues such as complexity, multiplicity of perspectives and human centredness. These issues can be more adequately addressed by narrative inquiry. For example, Carter argues for the usefulness of narrative in research on teaching and teacher education:

The special attractiveness of story in contemporary research on teaching and teacher education is grounded in the notion that story represents a way of knowing and thinking that is particularly suited to explicating the issues [teachers deal with].

(Carter, 1993, p. 6)

Elbaz (1990) lists six reasons why story is particularly fitting to make teachers' voices public:

1   Story relies on tacit knowledge to be understood.
2   It takes place in a meaningful context.
3   It calls on storytelling traditions which give structure to expression.
4   It often involves a moral lesson to be learnt.

5   It can voice criticism in socially acceptable ways.
6   It reflects the inseparability of thought and action in storytelling – the dialogue between the teller and the audience.

Polkinghorne (1988) points out the insufficiency of using statistical methods in seeking logical certainty of findings in human science research. He proposes that human sciences should also aim at producing results which are 'believable' and 'verisimilar'. He emphasises the fact that people often interpret statistical results to mean that the findings are important without considering 'the limited idea that the finding probably resulted from the chance drawing of sample elements from the population. In narrative research . . . a finding is significant if it is important' (Polkinghorne, 1988, p. 176).

Polkinghorne further argues that in quantitative research 'reliability' refers to the consistency and stability of the measuring instruments, whereas in narrative research it usually refers to the strength of the data analysis, in which attention is directed to the 'trustworthiness' of field notes and transcriptions of interviews. The goal of narrative analysis is to 'uncover the common themes or plots in the data. Analysis is carried out using hermeneutic techniques for noting underlying patterns across examples of stories' (Polkinghorne, 1988, p. 177).

Yoder-Wise and Kowalski (2003) list the key reasons for creating stories as

- *looking for recurring themes* – what actions have occurred that represent one's values, priorities, concerns, interests and experiences;
- *looking for consequences* – examining the cause and effect of choices that have been made;
- *looking for lessons* – what was learnt that influenced subsequent actions or behaviour;
- *looking for what worked* – recall and reflection on personal and professional successes; what were the essential contributing factors (e.g. timing, resources, vision);
- *looking for vulnerability* – identify any mistakes, failure to stimulate listeners to explore better approaches to problems;
- *building for future experiences* – how to create scenarios for handling certain situations; and
- *exploring other resources.*

Clandinin and Connelly (2000) perceive *emplotment, character, scene, place, time* and *point of view* as the central components of narrative. They contextualise narrative in the classroom in relation to teachers and define the narrative approach in comparison with traditional empirical approaches. They note that, through traditional methods, teachers are perceived as implementers of curricular programmes to meet preset objectives and achieve certain outcomes, whereas in narrative inquiry they are seen as a part of the curriculum, involved in establishing goals and making achievements.

Clandinin and Connelly (2000) point out major issues around which these approaches differ:

- temporality;
- context;
- people;
- action; and
- certainty.

In what Clandinin and Connelly call the 'grand narrative' (narrative of the traditional, empirical approaches, which dominated research for many decades), the studied phenomena are perceived as timeless, as they are at the time when they are studied, whereas in narrative inquiry *temporality* is a central feature. *Context* is ever present in narrative inquiry. It includes notions such as temporal context, spatial context and context of other people. Even though the 'grand narrative' acknowledges *context*, it essentially proceeds in a context-free way, attempting to create taxonomy that could be applied to all contexts.

For narrative inquiry, the curriculum, objectives and measurement of achievement need to reflect the *people* involved in them – teachers and students. The 'grand narrative' creates an essentially people-free notion. Narrative inquiry interprets curricular *actions* as classroom expressions of teachers' and students' narrative histories. Thus, as Connelly and Clandinin point out, a student's achievement in a test is a narrative sign of something, whereas the 'grand narrative' would perceive this as a direct evidence of the cognitive level obtained by the student. There is a sense of tentativeness in the narrative approach – the sense of doing 'one's best' under the circumstances, bearing in mind that there may be other possible interpretations. The traditional approaches attempt to develop *certainty*.

The traditional empirical and narrative approaches also differ in their regard of theory. Empirical research starts from theory; theory is designed as a structuring framework for the inquiry. However, narrative research forms a seamless link between the theory and practice embodied in the inquiry, and literature is used to enable conversation between theory and practice. Empirical research represents what Clandinin and Connelly (2000) term the 'god's eye' view of practice, while the narrative approach attempts to capture the 'multiplicity of voices' involved in creating the plotlines of stories.

Riessman (1993) highlights the fact that narrative does not sit neatly within the boundaries of any single scholarly field but that it is inherently interdisciplinary. She also points to the situatedness and interconnectedness of narratives: individuals' narratives are situated within particular interactions but also within social, cultural and institutional discourses, which should not be omitted in their interpretations.

Adler (1997) and Greenhalgh and Hurwitz (1999) underline the value of narrative approaches as an enhanced form of medical history taking. They argue that narrative approaches can assist the physician in formulating more appropriate diagnostic and treatment options, as well as improving doctor-patient relationships. Hellman (2005) acknowledges recent increases in illness narrative. Her explanation for this points to the humane side of the use of narrative approaches in medicine, but she also hints at the issue of complexity:

> [W]ith patients, this [the increase in illness narrative] may be because they need to reclaim their illness from our increasingly complex, technological and hospital-based health systems, which consider all illness within a bio-medical model.
>
> *(Hellman, 2005, p. 4)*

Greenhalgh and Hurwitz highlight the holistic nature of the narrative method:

> Understanding the narrative context of illness provides a framework for approaching a patient's problems holistically, as well as revealing diagnostic and therapeutic options.
>
> *(Greenhalgh and Hurwitz, 1999, p. 2)*

Similarly, Amsterdam and Bruner draw attention to the significance of narrative in law.

> Law lives on narrative. . . . For one, the law is awash in storytelling. Clients tell stories to lawyers. . . . As clients and lawyers talk, the client's story gets recast into plights and prospects . . . [and] judges and jurors retell the stories to themselves or to each other in the form of instructions, deliberations, a verdict, a set of findings, or an opinion. . . . This endless telling, casting and recasting is essential to the conduct of the law.
>
> *(Amsterdam and Bruner, 2000, p. 110)*

> Narrative . . . is the *necessary* discourse of law. . . . [R]ecognizing this . . . is an important step toward enriching the possibilities of storytelling in the legal process.
>
> *(Amsterdam and Bruner, 2000, p. 113)*

They point out the key features of narrative:

> [N]arrative and its forms do not sit quietly for the theorist bent on portraying them in the abstract. They are too value-laden, too multipurpose, too mutable and sensitive to context. . . . [N]arratives do pose interesting questions even if they are unable to yield answers.
>
> *(Amsterdam and Bruner, 2000, p. 115)*

They further argue that narrative is an essential part of human life in general.

> It seems almost as if humankind is unable to get on without stories. Knowing how to tell them and to comprehend them may be a part of the human survival kit. . . . [T]here appears to be something surreptitiously value-laden

> or value-promoting about storytelling. . . . Their [people's] stories give comfort, inspire, provide insight; they forewarn, betray, reveal, legitimize, convince.
> *(Amsterdam and Bruner, 2000, p. 114)*

These arguments indicate that, over the past nearly two decades, researchers from a widening range of disciplines have appreciated the value of narrative employed in both research and the practice of their disciplines. This stems from their realisation that scientific (traditional empirical) methods and tools on their own are increasingly not sufficient to deal with the complexity of human-centred issues they are faced with.

Summary

From a philosophical point of view, social sciences and educational research have been influenced most significantly by modernism, with its scientific perspective on research and its methodology. However, more recently, there has been a growing realisation of the need for a more holistic approach to address issues of complexity, multiplicity of perspectives and human centredness. Researchers from a wide range of disciplines (education, law, psychology, medicine) have proposed narrative inquiry as an alternative method which deals with such issues more adequately. This approach is in its essence closer to the philosophy of postmodernism. The researchers have highlighted the key features which make narrative inquiry more adequate in dealing with these issues. However, none of them has comprehensively described how to effectively use narrative inquiry as a research method across a range of disciplines. The following chapters endeavour to fulfil this task.

4

EXAMPLES OF STORIES IN NARRATIVE INQUIRY

Introduction to the stories

In the preceding three chapters we have outlined how and why we think narrative is important as a research method and described the origins and theoretical underpinnings of narrative. This chapter presents stories of actual research or teaching in which narrative has been utilised. These stories illustrate various uses of narrative in a range of fields, namely legal education, medical education, neurology, adult education, primary education, theology, social history and tertiary education. The stories are presented in the form of case studies. We first outline the discipline and context in which narrative has been used and then give samples of the individual stories. We start with a case study from our own teaching programme in a faculty of law (Story 1), in which narrative is employed as a means of reflection by programme participants on their professional practice and also as a form of evaluation of the programme.

In Story 2 the narrative research method is utilised to investigate a pilot programme in distance medical education, with the aim of improving similar medical educational programmes.

Story 3 is based on our recent interview with a colleague who has supervised a number of narrative-focused theses in the area of adult education.

Story 4 is a reflection by a senior lecturer in theology who uses narrative widely in his own research.

Story 5, based on Oliver Sacks' publication of stories from his neurological practice, underlines the significance of narrative in medical practice.

Story 6 deals with the issues of social justice in educating minority group children. In this story, narrative is employed to highlight the significant issues of social justice and to provide a means of resolving these issues.

In Story 7 narrative is utilised to paint a vivid picture of an era of British social history.

Story 8 relates some of the experiences of a Czech academic in the area of quality development in higher education.

The story excerpts are necessarily brief but include enough detail to provide at least a small taste of the flavour of each approach. The reader should approach these with the simple purpose of gaining an inkling of the different ways people use narrative methods.

Story 1: narrative inquiry in legal education

Discipline

Legal education.

Sources

'Reflective stories of course participants in a graduate certificate course in law teaching in 2003' (2003); 'Stories of professional practice' (2005).

Context of the story

Webster and Mertova ('Reflective stories of course participants in a graduate certificate course in law teaching in 2003', 2003) used narrative method in a pilot teacher professional development programme in the Faculty of Law. The programme was targeted at tertiary teachers of law and law-related disciplines and was carried out in a predominantly online distance learning mode, using specially designed flexible learning software. A narrative approach was used by asking the participants to reflect on their current teaching practices and the teaching and learning issues incorporated in the programme. A narrative method was also employed as a form of evaluation of the whole programme, in which the programme participants, as well as the educational developers who designed and taught the programme, were asked to write stories of experiences as a way of reflecting on the programme in order to assist its quality improvement.

The authors are of the view that reflective stories, as a form of evaluation, provide a holistic assessment of a programme. They can assist programme developers to identify critical aspects that require improvement or change better than, for instance, surveys incorporating multiple-choice questions that indicate degrees of programme participant satisfaction (ranging from highly positive to highly negative).

The following are samples of narrative reflections on the programme by two individuals: a law teacher (course participant) and an educational developer (teaching and developing the programme). They highlight which aspects of the programme they perceived to be significant.

Stories

A law teacher

From a personal point of view, self-reflection normally involves me in reviewing all the doubts I have about my teaching abilities. I question whether my teaching is really improving at all. Do I do enough to facilitate learning, or am I a boring, uninspiring teacher? I suppose this is the whole idea behind reflective practice, and I certainly hope that the process of worrying about these things ensures that I am a more effective teacher!

The taxonomies we looked at are a useful reminder of the ideals of teaching and learning. I know I tend to assume that I know what these ideals are, but if pressed I doubt if I would be able to express all the considerations in, for example, Bloom's taxonomy. So reviewing some of these theoretical checklists certainly helped me to reflect on what, why, and how I do things (or don't do things). Certainly, one thing the course has helped with is to suggest some ideas for alternative ways of conducting teaching and learning.

The subject's focus on learning outcomes forced me to actually think about what students should be taking out of courses, rather than simply focusing on my own teaching practices. This encouraged me to think quite critically about what law schools generally expect their students to learn, and how this measures up against my opinions of what life experiences students will have once they leave law school. There is a fundamental tension between these two expectations that I doubt will be resolved in the near future. Perhaps this needs to be a more express component of the subject. Assessment works the same way. I don't believe that exams are an effective form of assessment, yet they are so entrenched in law school culture in Australia.

Moving on from my reflections on some of the content of the course, I now want to consider my overall learning experience in this subject. First, I think the flexibility built into the subject was a bonus. Having the subject taught as an intensive certainly made it easier to fit into my schedule than would otherwise have been the case. The meetings were held at a good time, and seemed to be of an appropriate length for our purposes – that is, I think we were able to say everything we needed to say on each topic during the time provided.

I want to combine my reflections on the online aspect of the subject with our consideration of technology as a learning tool. I must admit I am very wary of the hype that surrounds promotion of technology as being automatically an improvement on, or different from, how things have been done in the past. In other words, technology must serve education, rather than the other way around . . .

An educational developer

It is now two years since I left the faculty. In looking back I have found the work I undertook there has been one of the primary influences on the way I operate in a different position in a different university with different staff.

If I was to note one particular characteristic that stood out in the complexities with which we were working, it was the simple nature of change and change resistance. My experience did not indicate that the challenges arose because, as developers, we were different and in many ways 'unknown' with regard to law but rather that academic tradition, and the generally perceived view of what an academic was, created far more resistance to our work than the factor of the discipline. I note this in reflection from my multiple experiences in an education faculty and currently working as a change agent. The work of educational development is extremely uncomfortable for a traditional academic who is used to dealing with the 'teaching' part simply through the passive transmission of content as a 'sage on the stage'. Flexible, online and alternative ways of teaching and learning take time, and often more time than the development and delivery of a passive content-focused one-hour lecture. In the eyes of the traditional academic, their priorities are research and other individual activities which will promote their name and reputation, with teaching being seen simply as a minor priority which they have to do in order to bring money into the faculty.

'Living' in a law faculty full-time, I think, would be different from being the 'part-time' visitor. In some ways, I 'lived' a chameleon life at that time. Many in my own education faculty were not quite sure what it was that I did. They could relate to my teaching responsibilities, and they knew I would always try and help them with 'technological' things, but for the most part the majority did not have real understanding of the nature of discipline teaching and learning per se. They too were predominantly disciplinary content specialists with the face-to-face mode of classroom presentation thrown in as the 'teaching method'. And this was perfectly understandable, as the classes they dealt with were primary and secondary education.

In relation to what I have said above, I never felt uncomfortable with the law lecturers. As a major strategy I have learnt over the years to be quite willing to play the role of the novice – and I was that when it came to the content. I would also play the role of the 'student' so that when they were delivering and developing, I would ask – as a student – what and how, etc. they intended for me to learn . . .

Yes, there were some who had no understanding of their students – but this was rare. And there were also times when some thought of us as glorified general administrative staff – but these were even fewer.

If I had one last comment, it would be that lawyers were in the main easier to work with than educators. They did not have the preconception that because I am an educator I am an expert in all things educational. They were willing to share and willing to learn . . . and I think in most cases enjoyed 'teaching' me!

Story 2: narrative research in medical education

Discipline

Medical education.

Source

Naidu and Cunnigton (2004).

Context of the story

Naidu and Cunnigton, working in a faculty of medicine, dentistry and health sciences, employed narrative inquiry in a research project to explore the experiences of staff and students with technology-enhanced teaching and learning. Their goal was to 'look beyond the existing, often rather superficial, data and closely examine how information and communication technology was influencing the nature of the teaching and learning transactions' (p. 141). They were particularly interested in the 'untold' stories and reflections of academics.

They sought insight into matters such as 'how approaches to teaching and learning are being impacted, how teacher thinking about teaching and learning is being modified, how students' approaches to learning are changing, and how student support is changing with the use of ICT [information and communications technology]' (p. 141). Naidu and Cunnigton highlighted the significance of narrative in reflection on professional practice and how it can subsequently lead to its improvement. They expressed a realisation that information and data derived from narrative inquiry 'are not easily generalisable to other contexts' (p. 153). They further pointed out that they expected to build a 'gallery' (i.e. a database of stories of academics' experience) over time with

> the amount of information and data that is necessary to draw conclusions and make meaningful generalisations. We anticipate that this gallery will grow into an extremely rich resource of the experience base of not only many pioneering efforts but some of the most innovative work that is being undertaken in this regard.
>
> *(pp. 153–154)*

The following is a sample of a reflection of a lecturer on using ICT in an innovative teaching project in the Faculty of Medicine, Dentistry and Health Sciences. The lecturer emphasised the significant aspects that the project brought to medical education and why such innovative approaches were vital.

Story

Medicine lecturer

> The new approach: (1) reduces dependence on factual knowledge; (2) enhances self-directed learning and communication skills of the students; (3) encourages integration of basic and clinical sciences; (4) introduces community-related issues and small group learning; and (5) introduces changes to assessment to match with the philosophy of the curriculum. This approach emphasises the need for formative assessment strategies, which this project addresses.
>
> *(p. 147)*

> I did not want to encourage rote learning but rather, use and application of knowledge, interpretation of data and clinical findings, decision making strategies and deeper understanding of the scientific basis of mechanisms and underlying pathophysiological processes. These important issues have no place in textbooks or lectures. . . . Deep understanding of these principles would not have been possible without the use of multimedia.
>
> *(p. 147)*

> We need to introduce innovative ways in the design and delivery of the curriculum. We need to use new ways to motivate our students to learn and search for new information.
>
> *(p. 151)*

> I think teachers need to move away from spoon-feeding students with information. You cannot feed them with every piece of information. . . . Instead we need to encourage self-directed learning and help students to do this. We need to challenge our students to move away from rote learning. . . .
> In this new approach to teaching and learning students are challenged to think, and we should continue to challenge them and enhance their abilities to link information, look for supportive evidence, make decisions and try to use information in solving problems.
>
> *(p. 152)*

> In medicine there are many times that you deal with uncertainty. . . . We need to prepare our students with strategies that enable them to deal with such uncertainty.
>
> *(p. 150)*

Story 3: narrative as a research method in education

Discipline

Adult education.

Source

'Reflection on narrative by Dr Sue McNamara' (2005).

Context of the story

This case consists of an edited extract of an interview we carried out with a colleague who has supervised a number of theses using narrative in the field of education. She perceived narrative as a powerful holistic research tool to deal with the issues of complexity and human and cultural centredness. She was of the view that narrative as a research method is much more 'honest' and closer to reality than most empirical methods.

Story

Senior lecturer in education

Not all of those I have worked with would describe narrative perhaps in the same way. Most of those who have come to research have had it in their mind to begin with a qualitative study and won't have heard of the idea of stories or narrative. . . . Most researchers with whom I've worked were probably using more common research terms than even the word 'narrative'. Most of them have come in talking about doing a case study, action research, an autoethnography or different variations on the theme of qualitative research . . . and the idea of narrative has become more of a reporting mechanism for their study than a methodology, in its own right, for many of them, because they've come across it once they have decided on their area.

The idea of narrative does arise from the idea of the descriptive, and it is far more holistic than the scientific approach, which narrows down to one or more elements. The idea of narrative is a culmination of bringing together the myriad of chaotic elements that you find in a study, and it doesn't place more emphasis on one than the other. . . .

Narrative is closer to reality, it captures the culture. . . . I think it's richer than a lot of other methods. It probably does take much more training to do it properly than it does to do quantitative research, but it's more honest. . . . And narrative inquiry is more a reflective process, but a reflective process looking for inspiration. . . . Narrative inquiry to me is often retrospective.

One project is the story of the development of a naturopathic college in New Zealand. The lady who undertook the research was taking a personal journey, and she was looking at putting her narrative together – all the influences and factors that built up . . . sometimes over a twenty-year period. . . . The actual focus of her study was on how you help distance learning students to stay with a course. . . . What she ended up doing was tracking the whole development of an organisation, which specialised in that area. . . . [A]nd the more she used it as a research tool, the more she unfolded the complexity of what she was looking at.

Another one [project] that's being done now is looking at students crossing cultures, students learning languages to operate in a global world when they come from an Eastern tradition.

Another one [project] that we are in the very initial stages of now is the stories of teachers' experiences. What we are trying to do is to see how their stories can give us guidance for designing, developing and implementing professional development in a technology-based environment. And we want to see if others can learn from the stories of their experience, and if we can capture it in a multimedia way, if it can give us guidance to what we really need to be looking at for teachers and learners. We need to give them a different mindset, and changing mindset is like trying to change a culture.

Story 4: narrative in different cultural contexts

Discipline

Theology.

Source

'Reflection on narrative by Dr Les Henson' (2006).

Context of the story

The following is the case of a missionary who has spent a long period of time abroad, in a cultural context very different from his own (Australian). He has subsequently undertaken a master's degree and later a PhD in the field of theology using narrative inquiry as the research method. Following is his story summarising what motivated him to use narrative in his research.

Story

My journey with narrative

My journey with narrative began as a result of my long-term involvement with the Momina people of the southern lowlands of West Papua, Indonesia. I lived and worked among the Momina from 1978 to 1995 as a cross-cultural missionary. It was in this capacity that I encountered the power, mystery and enchantment of narrative and eventually narrative as a research methodology. In researching the culture, worldview and traditional religion of the Momina, I slowly began to recognise that the epistemological foundations of their world were narratively orientated. Rather than convey foundational truth and meaning in the abstract form of propositions they, unlike many Westerners, communicated the essential truths and foundational meanings that held society together in the narrative form of story and ritual.

In studying the Momina spirit cosmology as part of my Masters programme I became fascinated by the interconnectedness and integrating capacity of deep-level worldview themes, like life, death, community, harmony and reciprocity. These worldview themes, and their accompanying surface-level motifs, flowed through the cultural subsystems and deep into the heart of their worldview like the flavours of a Neapolitan ice cream. Yet they were most powerfully observed in the Momina myths, folktales, spirit beings and feasts with their accompanying rituals.

After establishing the surface-level motifs of the Momina worldview core theme of life, on which I focused, I proceeded to develop a method for bringing the cultural context and the biblical text together, so that the life motifs could be developed in an appropriate biblical, theological and contextual manner. In doing so, I realised the need to use a narrative approach to theologising because of the oral nature and narrative orientation of Momina society.

Several years later, while completing my PhD, which focused upon a model for doing contextual theology in Melanesia, I employed a narrative case study methodology at the heart of my research. Three core chapters developed a personal narrative that reflected upon my journey in helping the Momina and describing the process of the development of a contextual theology in their midst. The purpose of these chapters was twofold. First, it provided a concrete case of the development of a contextual theology to test my theoretical conclusions with respect to the process of developing contextual theology. Second, in reflecting on the narrative case study, conclusions were drawn with respect to methodological principles and criteria for assessing the doing of contextual theology within the Melanesian context.

The case study described and reflected upon the methods and approaches used in the development of theology among the Momina. It placed the development process in the context of my interaction with the Momina people and the growth of the Momina church. Consequently, these chapters used my 'personal pilgrimage to shape and inform' the missiological process, putting flesh on the bones of theory and encouraging an integrative process of missiological reflection. Consequently, my journey into narrative has been very much aligned with my involvement with the Momina people and their journey in understanding their new-found faith.

The two ways I have used narrative in my research involved differing degrees of complexity. The use of myth and folktale required both myth and worldview analysis methodologies and theological reflection, while the use of a personal narrative case study was more of a reflective storytelling experience in which I was deeply and personally involved. It provided a concrete means of validating and testing the theories developed in other sections of my thesis. I used such approaches because of their contextual appropriateness to the projects and the academic disciplines in which I was operating. Myths and folktales were compiled by recording Momina storytellers and my personal narrative case study was developed from personal letters, journals, records and papers I had written over a period of 18 years. Authors who have helped and influenced me on this journey are many, but Geertz's use of 'thick' descriptions and Goldberg's approach to theology and narrative have been influential. I would advocate the use of narrative methodology because it enlivens what can easily become dead, lifeless theory and, at times, boring research. From the Momina I have learnt that abstract theory is best enfleshed in concrete forms of story and ritual.

Story 5: narrative in clinical practice

Discipline

Medicine – neurology.

Source

Sacks (1998).

Context of the story

This story is taken from a book by Oliver Sacks called *The Man Who Mistook His Wife for a Hat and Other Clinical Tales*. In the preface, Sacks highlights the value of clinical stories for medical practice. He points out that 'richly human clinical tales' reached their climax in the nineteenth century and then interest in them gradually declined as an 'impersonal neurological science' emerged.

Sacks believed that narrative has an important place in medicine, even in the current times, and that something is missing in the purely scientific approach to medicine. Sacks' book incorporates a number of stories, giving a rich picture of each of his neurological cases. The book underlines the fact that stories of professional practice are an important means of educating other practitioners from both the same field and outside the field. The following is a sample of a story in which Sacks described one of his cases. First, Sacks gave the background of his neurological case and showed his immediate reaction to the neurological disorder of his patient during the patient's first visit. Then he further reflected on his patient's disorder some time later and indicated how the case had developed. In the last extract, Sacks points to the importance of taking account of the human factors (judgements and feelings) in neurology and that to consider only the scientific aspects of individual neurological cases, as is frequently done, is not sufficient.

Story

Dr P. was a musician of distinction, well known for many years as a singer, and then, at the School of Music, as a teacher. It was here in relation to his students, that certain strange problems were first observed. Sometimes a student would present himself, and Dr P. would not recognize him; or, specifically, would not recognize his face. The moment the student spoke, he would be recognized by his voice. Such incidents multiplied, causing embarrassment, perplexity, fear – and, sometimes, comedy. For not only did Dr P. increasingly fail to see faces, but he saw faces when there were no faces to see. . . .

At first these odd mistakes were laughed off as jokes, not least by Dr P. himself. . . .

The notion of there being 'something the matter' did not emerge until some three years later, when diabetes developed. Well aware that diabetes could affect his eyes, Dr P. consulted an ophthalmologist, who took a careful history and examined his eyes closely. 'There's nothing the matter with your eyes,' the doctor concluded. 'But there is trouble with the visual parts of your brain. You don't need my help[;] you must see a neurologist.' And so, as a result of this referral, Dr P. came to me.

It was obvious within a few seconds of meeting him that there was no trace of dementia in the ordinary sense. He was a man of great cultivation and charm who talked well and fluently, with imagination and humour. I couldn't think why he had been referred to our clinic.

And yet there *was* something a bit odd. He faced me as he spoke, was oriented towards me, and yet there was something the matter – it was difficult to formulate. He faced me with his *ears*. . . .

(pp. 8–9)

How should one interpret Dr P.'s peculiar inability to interpret, to judge, a glove as a glove? [When given a glove by Dr Sacks, the patient couldn't work out what that was.] Manifestly, here, he could not make a cognitive judgment, though he was prolific in the production of cognitive hypotheses. A judgment is intuitive, personal, comprehensive, and concrete – we 'see' how things stand, in relation to one another and oneself. It was precisely this setting, this relating, that Dr P. lacked (though his judging, in all other spheres, was prompt and normal). Was this due to lack of visual information, or faulty processing of visual information? (This would be the explanation given by a classical, schematic neurology.) Or was there something amiss in Dr P.'s attitude, so that he could not relate what he saw to himself?

(p. 19)

Of course, the brain *is* a machine and a computer – everything in classical neurology is correct. But our mental processes, which constitute our being and life, are not just abstract and mechanical, but personal, as well – and, as such, involve not just classifying and categorizing, but continual judging and feeling also. If this is missing, we become computer-like, as Dr P. was.

(p. 20)

Story 6: social justice in educating minority groups

Discipline

Primary education.

Source

Shields *et al.* (2005).

Context of the story

This story is taken from a book by Shields *et al.* published in 2005. The book describes a research project investigating minority children's education in the United States, New Zealand and Israel. (The investigated minority group in the United States is the Navajo; in New Zealand, it is the Maori; and in Israel, it is the Bedouin.) The authors employ a narrative inquiry method, with particular focus on discourse, to investigate social justice issues in minority children's education in their respective countries.

In the authors' own words, their book

> is an exploration of how schooling creates and perpetuates images of children in ways that are destructive, in ways that predispose some children to be successful, confident, and engaged, and others to become lower achievers, timid or aggressive, reluctant, and disengaged.
>
> *(p. xxiii)*

For Shields *et al.* the narratives of the students, teachers, administrators and parents were a powerful means of uncovering the issues, which the students, teachers and others considered significant for minority children's education.

They further argued that stories of experience also had a significant potential for change.

> New positionings make available to teachers different concepts, metaphors, images and language. Teachers can then re-story their experiences and take on different ways of seeing the world as their own. . . . [A] profound change will involve more than just technical changes of strategies, and/or interaction patterns. There will also be an emotional and a conceptual aspect to the changes as repositioning affects our sense who we are.
>
> *(p. 148)*

The following are a few stories of the sorts of issues discussed in the narratives Shields *et al.* have collected in their research.

Stories

Administrator, United States

Not all bilingual programs feel safe for the students. For many the program is something that is being done to them because it has been decided by the curriculum committee because of the law suit. It is not a bilingual program in the sense that it offers true bilingual education. Our program is a restorative model. Restoring the Navajo language to students. In many cases parents are withdrawing their children because they either don't care for the teachers or the instruction or do not want their children to speak Navajo because of their poor experience in Boarding school. I myself support bilingual instruction. Our model is not accomplishing developing a language base on which students can develop literacy.

(p. 43)

Teacher, New Zealand

Our children [Maori students] are quite aboriginal in their behaviours outside of school . . . just like a pack of wolves . . . some really tough little hombres, they needle adults including me. Once I'm outside of this school, I'm fair game just like any other person in this town. When it comes back into school they quite often have trouble adjusting their behaviour. . . . [T]his is the huge contributor to the down side of learning.

(p. 75)

Teacher, Israel

I am frustrated when I enter the classroom during the day and I know that these pupils, who are seated in front of me, arrived to school without energy, without motivation, and they live in really sub-human conditions.

(p. ix)

Teacher, New Zealand

They go backward and forward depending on what is happening in their families. Stay with aunties, then go back home. . . . Transient to a certain extent that they go backwards and forwards. I think the young Maori students here are more transient than perhaps the other cultural groups.

(p. 75)

Maori student, New Zealand

I think part of the difficulties we have in the teaching world, like all the rest of the world, is that we don't have common values at the moment.

(p. 77)

A Bedouin teacher, Israel

Somebody [else] determines what we should teach. It has to do with politics. Let's say [the] history of our people, I can't teach [it] in school. . . . The Ministry of Education determines this for me. Our aspirations, we should be let to build our own curriculum, in Arabic, religion, history. . . . The [current] curriculum is very weak. If we travel to a neighbouring country we will see that we don't know any Arabic. Regarding history, I know that minorities all over the world build their own curricula. We don't, we can't.

(p. 100)

A non-Bedouin teacher, Israel

[T]he child is not relaxed. . . . Let us make [the following] comparison: the relaxed child would have spoken to you fluently. The non-relaxed child or the one who fears you . . . [gives] the shortest possible answers, if any. And you can just see it whether this child who is eight years old or ten . . . has already received some education of self-confidence, whether he would stand and talk with you or not.

(p. 103)

A Bedouin teacher, Israel

Some wanted to become a physician, some wanted to become – like me – . . . [a] teacher; really a great part. Some wanted to be engineers, and some girls – lawyers. All kinds of, very diversified. Some wanted to be scientists in the stars. . . . Some [say]: I want to be a pilot. I know that any non-Jew cannot become a pilot. So, I let the child live with this illusion. When he will be an adult, he will face that. . . . It frustrates me, but I can't . . . express my opinion. I can't [tell] that child who is [just] starting his way, when he dreams about something, that he can't [realise it]. Perhaps when he graduates from high school, things [will have] changed [by then].

(p. 115)

Story 7: social changes in Britain during the 1950s and 1960s

Discipline

Social history/cultural studies.

Source

Akhtar and Humphries (2001).

Context of the story

This story is taken from a book by Akhtar and Humphries on the lifestyle changes people in Britain experienced in the 1950s and 1960s. The book was written chronologically, with each chapter dealing with a particular new cultural/social trend occurring in that era. Every chapter tells of a particular cultural/social trend and is interwoven with personal stories of those who experienced the 1950s and 1960s in Britain. It appears that Akhtar and Humphries have chosen the form of stories for individual chapters and their sections, interwoven with authentic personal stories quite intuitively. We assume that this was because this form of narrative best suited their purposes, and the personal stories have made the narrative more vivid.

Stories

Dream homes

In the summer of 1951 millions of people visited the Festival of Britain, a government-sponsored extravaganza on the south bank of the Thames in London. On 27 acres of bomb-scarred wasteland some of the best architects of the country had built a miniature wonderland, a vision of the new Britain that would rise out of the ashes of the war.

(p. 55)

Even before the war there had been a shortage of decent housing, but now the combined effects of bomb damage, a flood of returning soldiers and the baby boom made the lack of homes a desperate problem for the government. Most official estimates admitted a shortage of around four million homes, and over a quarter of a million families were forced to live in buildings that were unfit for human habitation. Many were newly married who lived with relatives or in cramped furnished rooms. For several years after the war Gina Spreckley lived in north London with her husband and two small children. 'We had rooms in a house belonging to a relative. We only took it because there was nothing else. The whole house was crumbling. Every time you shut a door hard a bit of the ceiling fell down. Big mushrooms the size of breakfast plates grew up the walls, and if you cut them down in a few days they grew back again. There was a hole in the bedroom floor a foot square where the rats gnawed away. My daughter had asthma because of the conditions. And we had no privacy, no bathroom of our own . . .'

(p. 56)

All mod cons

The coming of electricity was treated as a milestone, and the excitement was so great that some people proudly showed off their naked light bulbs. Jo Jones was a teenager growing up in rural Flintshire when electricity arrived in her village. 'We were told it was coming in twelve months' time so we had the whole house wired with these thick grey cables crawling round the rooms, and lived in huge anticipation of the great switch-on. My friends had it for months before we finally got it. It was fantastic when it arrived, you could have light on wherever you wanted it. . . . It worked out really well because we didn't have that "being on top of one another feeling" any more.' Having electricity expanded the living space in the home. People were no longer confined to one room for heat and light and the whole house was opened up to them.

(p. 81)

In Britain the first generation [of women] to enjoy household technology en masse was also the first to have benefited from an extended secondary education. Many of these women felt they had good brains going to rust and having the mod cons enabled them to escape the bondage of the home and spread their wings a little. The automated appliances saved time and effort and enabled women to turn away from the housework to other things, be it further education, a job or simply more of a life outside the home. In Christine Fagg's case, mod cons had major impact on her life. 'My trouble was that I wanted desperately to do things outside my home and all the time I was reaching out and struggling to educate myself further. I was always trying to think of short cuts to the housework, to get out and stimulate my own interests, and that's where the washing machine, the Hoover, etc really came into their own. As the years rolled by and the children were growing up, I had no career, no qualifications and so I knew I must prepare for something. At this time they had just started to run courses for adults at colleges of further education . . . '

(p. 93)

The car's the star

'It was treated like the crown jewels. The car came out just once a week on a Sunday,' remembers Dorothy Robson from her fifties childhood in Oswaldtwistle, Lancashire. 'Dad would take us all out for a spin, then wash it and put it in the garage again.' The 1950s saw the start of motoring mania in Britain. Having a car was a source of pride, a status symbol and a sign of affluence in an age of prosperity. The car – once only available to the wealthiest – came within the reach of the average family as mass-produced vehicles started to roll off production lines. Having a motor was a passport to freedom. The Sunday drive, the weekend away, the holiday, the house in the country, away from the office, commuting, all became possible with an independent set of wheels. From the beginning of the fifties to the end of the sixties the number of cars on the roads increased tenfold.

(p. 149)

Story 8: narrative inquiry in quality in higher education

Discipline

Higher education.

Source

'Stories of academics in higher education quality' (2006).

Context of the story

This story captures some experiences of the head of an office for international studies at a university in the Czech Republic with quality development in higher education. The story excerpts provided here are drawn from an interview for a research project that employed narrative inquiry as a research method and demonstrate the revealing nature of stories in giving us direct insights into different educational issues and problems that can arise. This story deviates in structure from previous stories in that it not only records specific events but engages in presenting some reasons for the context in which the story is told.

The topic of the story, quality development in higher education, has gained attention in higher education institutions worldwide. There have been various responses to this trend, ranging from implementing direct quality measurement scales to conducting self-audits. Increasingly, the rationale for quality development has been driven by funding mechanisms, accreditation tests, keeping pace with international practice, national audits and other general trends, such as the massive growth in higher education and the influence of information technology.

However, it can be argued that the 'human factor' involved in quality development is equally important as, if not more so than, institutional and political imperatives. Thus, the aim of this story is to capture that human factor through the experiences of an individual involved in the process of quality development in the Czech Republic. Further, it briefly highlights the issues and struggles of dealing with change in the context of worldviews that have been formed in different political and social contexts.

Story of the head of an office for international studies (Czech Republic)

Since 2000 I've been the head of an Office for International Studies at this university. This is our main office for international relations at the university, and was created in 2000 in an attempt to centralise all the various aspects of international relations. We don't include international links and research, as such, but all the other aspects: teacher and student mobility, programmes in English, doctoral degree programmes, other domestic programmes for international students, presentation of the university abroad, bilateral agreements – all of these. . . .

In 2004/2003 we were involved in an evaluation which is run by the European University Association (EUA), and it is specifically an evaluation of quality, quality development and the quality mechanism. It is extremely complex because it involves preparation of an internal self-evaluation report, and then a first visit by people from the EUA, and then preparation of more materials for them and then a second visit by them, after which they then make their final report. We were completely in charge of that and I was the one who ended up writing the self-evaluation report for the university – so it involved me in quite a lot of work more directly related to evaluation and quality evaluation. . . .

The EUA is an interesting example of the kind of standard that is being spread over Europe. They give you a very clear set of guidelines by which you have to prepare the self-evaluation. At that time, when the rector had to nominate a team from all faculties and different institutions to work on the report, we got together and there were two key things. One is that people said that they felt they were not competent to talk about this, which is one of the problems in this culture, and it is that everybody is, or thinks they are, highly specialised in one little area, and 'I've never heard about quality, then I can't talk about it.' And then the other thing was, of course, that they thought that quality would be measured in numbers. And one of our vice rectors said: 'That isn't a problem – we had 20,000 students five years ago, we have 30,000 students, we got X million crowns in grants for research, and so quality must be good.' So I said: 'Well, maybe we've got twice as many students so the quality of teaching is only half as good.' And they couldn't understand it, because they are so used to quantifying things in this way due to the old communist system: the more, the better. . . .

Once I said: 'No, that's not what we are talking about, we are talking about something much more elusive.' Virtually all of them said: 'Well, we don't think that we are competent enough to do what is expected of us.' And so, in fact, when it came to writing the report, we did it virtually backwards in a sense, on the basis of what I knew about the university and what I've talked to people about, then they commented on the report and added things.

Another thing about quality and quality assessment is that people in this culture are not used to – when it comes to talk about quality – publicly saying anything other than good things. And that's interesting, because I wrote the report as I saw the university with strong points, weak points and so on. And this was actually quite positively received by the evaluators, when they came.

There's a tendency in this culture illustrated by that story about the monk who is seeking to be enlightened. He's never enlightened and he walks by a butchers' shop and there's a customer in the butchers' shop and the customer says to the butcher that he'd like to buy the best cut of meat and the butcher says: 'All of my cuts are the best.' And at this moment the monk is enlightened. And I think that in the Czech university culture there is a tendency to say: 'Everything we do is the best.' And so quality ceases to have any kind of meaning. . . .

After the changes in 1989, I was elected the head of the English department, and my primary concern right away was to change the whole structure of the studies, and to change teaching and evaluation methods in order to improve the quality. For me, this meant first of all much less emphasis on rote learning, much less emphasis on this idea of compactness of knowledge, much more emphasis on thinking, interpreting, which meant, of course, openness to theory. . . .

So my primary concern at that stage as head of the department was to improve the quality of teaching – of the courses, the options, the variety of the courses, and the way they were being examined – to improve the quality of the student we were producing. And I underestimated the other aspect, which was the quality of teachers' professional development, doctorates, further degrees and so on.

Before 1989, we had first of all a Fulbrighter each year, then we had someone from the British Council, and it was clear that these people were coming from a richer academic culture. But that was something that you would pick up from talking in a pub in the evening or something like that. After 1989, by which time I had been elected head of an English department, we had more of these people and, as we set about trying to change the curriculum, I was concerned that they should be a part of it, and this was perhaps the most radical decision that included quality that I've ever taken. There was a great deal of opposition on the part of many of the Czech teachers in the department – not all of them but many of them. They said: 'This is our teaching programme; why should we include foreigners in this revision of our teaching programme?' I said: 'Look we have to admit that we've been cut off for a long time.' But it turned into a process – it took about two years. It was a long process because I wanted everybody to feel that they had some stake in the final changes – that they've had an input, that their view has been listened to, discussed, perhaps taken on board.

It became clear early on in those discussions that it was a huge change that was going to take place. Some of the changes I've anticipated before because they've been based on my own experience of being educated in Canada and Britain in the 1960s, but that was 30 or 25 years before.

But the forming of this critical route that was for the first time part of our discussion – Where do we go? How do we change? What do we create? – was certainly in my eyes the change that was needed. It was not a tinkering with things, it was not introducing an element A, and element B, but it was a total restructure of the whole programme in ways that were felt by many of the Czech teachers as radical and threatening.

It was the process of transforming of the curriculum as a department, which was the moment at which I became aware that we had to do things very differently.

In terms of the things we are involved in at the present time, if I say there's a battle going on, perhaps that's not true, because now we are talking about internationalisation. To me, internationalisation is a quality measure because it's got so many aspects which relate to quality. One aspect of it is our vague aim to have many more international students in the university. But, of course, how are we going to get them? Are we going to encourage them to come here and study in Czech? There is one group of people at the university who think that we can recruit heavily from places like Slovakia, Russia and Serbia. Slovaks can study here with no problems, the others with a short intensive course in Czech, and we can attract very good students this way. There's another group that says no, the only real way is to move significantly towards English language programmes – not BA programmes, but certainly MA and doctoral programmes. There is an implication for quality there, because I think that you are going to be much more aware of your quality if you are creating English language programmes – suddenly you are in a total internationally competitive network. If you are saying we want the best students to do our degrees in Czech, basically what we are saying is that our degrees in Czech are better than their degrees there. Basically, this is saying that we don't have to change, because we assume that they want to come here, they want to learn so that they can get a degree in the Czech Republic. This may well be. I mean, for many of these countries they are talking about, in terms of a prospective career and so on, it probably is more attractive to study here than there but, to me, there is a kind of uncosted element of self-satisfaction, and there is not much question of quality.

If they are going to start any kind of degree in English, whether it's one of your own or it's joint with another university, immediately you are up against the question of whether it's going to be good enough to compete with all the others out there. So, there are discussions going on, I mean, we are moving, but very slowly.

I think a part of the reluctance of some people to introduce English degrees is an unconscious, sort of nagging doubt whether we are good enough. Is our teachers' English good enough? Part of it is on a deeper level: Is our capacity good enough to offer an attractive degree that will compete internationally?

To me, this promotion of English-language degree programmes is deeply linked with the question of quality and it's something that I've only become aware of recently. I thought, OK, we want to attract students to do English-language programmes, but then I've realised the implications, particularly in the area of quality, doubts, etc.

One of our faculties has introduced two MA programmes in English. They are two-year programmes and their first students are graduating now. Those students are involved in a very intense and delicate discussion with the faculty, pointing out to them where they think the degrees could be improved, where these were not as good as they had hoped and so on. To give the faculty credit, they are treating this extremely seriously, and it is an open dialogue, which I think is extraordinary because it would be so easy to say: 'Well, OK, thank you for your opinion.' But they do seem to be taking this very seriously and, essentially, what these people are commenting on is quality.

We are doing the same thing in the summer school we run, and there is a one-semester Central European Studies programme, which is a selection of individual courses in English dealing with the region. We ask students for feedback: the material that is dealt with, the kind of teaching, etc.

So, I think that in the Czech context at the moment English language programmes are an interesting way of improving quality where quality is essential, and this is not the quality of their English, because they are offering these courses to people who are used to a different kind of teaching; these students are used to a different way of learning.

Another example of quality relates to our starting a Canadian Studies Association for Central Europe and it has people from countries all over central Europe. Central Europe is defined as Poland in the north, Serbia in the south, Bulgaria and Romania in the east – so it's quite a large concept of central Europe. One of the things that we've decided is that we wanted a journal, and our first question was: How do we create this journal? Right from the beginning I said: 'Well, we've got to think of this as a serious scholarly journal.' We knew what the problem was going to be. Because it's central Europe, because professors are used to having their articles published when they send them in, and professors are used to promoting their students, they get their articles to be published. We devised what seems to be a very time-consuming and clumsy measure: every article that is submitted is read by four people from four different countries. This is a huge amount of work, a huge amount of reading, we've got a scale by which they can judge things, all the reviews are put together and then we make decisions, or the editor makes decisions, and then the article gets accepted, it's rejected or it's sent back for a rewrite. This quality control mechanism was put in from the very beginning, and it was very interesting because, with the very first issue, we knew exactly what would happen. We got these articles from various people; it aroused immense ire and anger on the part of certain prominent people. We were able to say: 'Look, we have this objective that it's read by four people, and sorry, this is just not good enough.' End of discussion. And, I think, the quality is good now, and has been from the beginning because of that. This is an example of how you sometimes have to put a lot of work into something when you are serious about quality. Quality is time consuming, or assuring quality is time consuming. But it works quite well. This is just another example of an area where because of local circumstances you may have to do odd things to achieve the quality control.

We do this in all our Canadian Studies stuff, when there are scholarship grants to Canada and so on. We have a different committee each year meeting. It's a funny system with these Canadian Studies. We read the applications – we are actually a pre-selection committee – and then we send them with all our comments to Ottawa, and they make the final decisions in Ottawa, which are 95 per cent the same as us, sometimes a little bit different. In fact, it's another quality control mechanism.

What we've also done, which nobody else has done, is that, when the results come out, we actually write to each of the people who didn't get the grant explaining where the weak points were, and where they should be careful next year, if they apply again. Sometimes, even if people do get the grant, if they were a bit weak, but still got the grant, we write to them saying: 'You got the grant, congratulations, as a plus thing the weak point was this.' We are very concerned about this, but it takes an effort, and nobody else does this. You got the grant or you didn't, that's it, end of discussion. So, we felt this was necessary because, generally, in the central European region, people don't understand these standards; people don't know what these international levels of quality are. Generally, people here are just starting to talk about quality, and it's really just starting from scratch, and sometimes you have to point out things that are quite obvious.

One of the problems of quality and assuring quality is that partly it requires establishing mechanisms, like for people reviewing it and so on, which for some Czechs is just more bureaucracy. They don't appreciate the positive ways some mechanisms can work in achieving quality for all applicants or achieving certain standards. They underestimate the importance of this sort of thing.

Only now are we starting to introduce some sort of mechanisms. There is no mechanism for the university for judging the quality of teaching. There's a kind of mechanism which is that students fill in questionnaires, and those actually have a function. The people from the EUA asked whether they work. And they do. The students, at the end, if they wish to, can fill in a little evaluation form of the course they've taken.

We have an information system, and it works in a very clever way now. When you are deciding on what kind of courses to take for the next semester, you can look at the student evaluation made by other students, but only if you yourself have filled in the evaluation for the courses you've taken. Very simple, but very clever mechanism, so one of the results is that something like 60 per cent of the students do the evaluation of the courses. And there's a whole hierarchy: an ordinary teacher can see only the evaluation of his or her courses, the head of the department can see everybody else's from his/ her department, the dean can see the evaluations of the whole faculty and the rector can see the whole university, or the rector and the vice rector for study. Heads of departments and deans regularly look at these things, and they make suggestions, they talk to teachers, and if, after two or three semesters, the same problem or the same teacher is coming up, teachers are shifted or taken away from that course into other courses, or teachers have been let go. Teachers have been let go, because it's clear that the quality is not good enough. This is one mechanism we have introduced. Otherwise, we don't have many others.

There is no mechanism whatsoever for judging the quality of administrative workers employed by the university. Even if some things have been introduced as a part of our internationalisation strategy, for instance, all of the jobs in the university have an added language component put into them. We looked at all the jobs at the university and considered what degree of English would be necessary. If we want to be an international university, what level of English does a librarian need, what level of English does a departmental secretary need? This is now all a part of the job description. When jobs are advertised, people either have to have reached that level already or have to reach it within a certain time after coming here. We have internal English language classes, which are free, as a part of the career development of the employees.

So we are moving in this direction now, and we have actually introduced one senior position at the rector's office for creating quality mechanisms at the university. It is happening here, largely as a result of the EUA evaluation.

Quality evaluation of research programmes – there is something of that as well. There is a whole series of projects called development projects from the ministry. It used to be that we sent it in and that was it. Now what they do is, every year, they've got an internal mechanism that requires you to come, report and be questioned on it by a special board. They've discovered some interesting issues between the report and what actually happened in a few instances. They are trying in these kinds of ways to improve quality. We are moving in that direction but it's a slow process, especially in this culture. People react against the communist years, and have the sense that any attempt to check up on you is limiting your freedom.

I'll give you an interesting example of this. When we introduced our new curriculum in the English department, it included a large part of optional courses, but this then, of course, created a question of how teachers should mark. Unfortunately, there were some teachers in the department who gave virtually nothing but As, while others were very strict. I knew exactly what was going to happen – weak students would seek out these easy teachers. It improved in the 1990s, but it was still there with certain teachers, and at one of the department meetings I said: 'Well, you must realise that we've simply moved to this model, and it has other implications that I've explained. I'm obviously not going to tell you that you've got to have 5 per cent first class, 16 per cent second and so on, but there has to be some sort of general consensus on marking, and yet you may have an exceptionally clever, or sometimes exceptionally dumb, group of students.' But these were extremes where one teacher was giving no As and hardly any Bs and only Cs and Ds, and someone else only As. It's not fair on the students as a whole. Some people got a very easy education, and others a difficult one – the ones that got it difficult were going to get a better education, but still. Some people get a wonderful record, and other people get weaker one, and yet these people are better students. One of our senior member of the department got up literally raving, saying: 'I got 40 years of communists telling me what I could do, where is academic freedom – I can mark the way I want, nobody is going to tell me how I can mark.' And so on and so on.

One of the problems is that quality control also means generally accepted standards; it is essential to what is acceptable and what isn't. A lot of people, especially the older generation, find it absolutely impossible to understand. Especially now, when you work towards the European standards system, where the number of credits for courses is supposed to reflect the weight of the course – not for sitting in the class for X hours, but how much reading is required, the difficulty of the exams or other evaluation methods, and so on. You've got to have generally accepted standards, and many teachers still cannot grasp this. They still think that the teacher is a god, and can do what he or she wants, and that's got nothing to do with the department, the faculty, or whatever else. That's their concept of academic freedom. I could give you lots of examples of stuff like that. Quality control is very difficult to introduce in this culture for many reasons.

Summary

The stories in this chapter provide examples of how narrative has been employed in a range of different disciplines and represent various ways and purposes for which stories can be utilised. In Stories 1 and 2, narrative provides a means of reflection on innovative teaching practices in law and medicine/psychiatry. It further presents a learning/teaching tool for reflecting on the current professional practices of programme participants and provides a means of evaluation in order to further develop teaching practices and materials. Story 3 is a contemplation on how and why researchers in the field of adult education come to choose narrative. Story 4 reflects on the significance of narrative in dealing with aspects of cultural difference through theological practice. Story 5 presents an argument for the significance of the story as a means of conveying issues in neurological practice. Story 6 relates to the field of primary education where stories of students and teachers highlight the issues of social justice (or injustice) regarding minority group students and help in looking for solutions to these issues. In Story 7, personal stories are utilised to create a more vivid and authentic picture of social changes in Britain in the 1950s and 1960s. In Story 8, narrative is employed to highlight significant aspects of higher education quality in the Czech Republic.

Researchers or practitioners in various fields have elected to use narrative to provide a more holistic picture of the issues of their concern, to help them reveal and better deal with the complexities of those issues. By using narrative, they also highlight the human centredness of professional practice and research, as well as making their stories more interesting. The authors of this book argue that narrative tends to highlight critical episodes and events and in so doing provides insights into human understanding, as well as manageable ways of focusing on outcomes and recommendations for improvement. In the following chapters we deal with the utility of critical events and episodes in narrative in more detail.

5

A CRITICAL EVENTS APPROACH
TO NARRATIVE

This chapter proposes that narrative can be analysed through the highlighting and capturing of critical events contained in stories of experience. Narrative sketches detailing place, time, characters and events assist the researcher in identifying the critical event. Data sources, which inform these narrative sketches, include surveys, observations, documentation and interviews that enhance the time, place and description of the critical event. The collection of this data provides researchers with a holistic view of their investigation and enables them to classify occurrences into critical and supporting events, which are often overlooked or not revealed through traditional empirical methods. These events then become reportable findings and outcomes of the research.

Narrative and critical events

The previous chapter established the educational underpinning of narrative in research and teaching. This chapter focuses on the use of critical events revealed within stories of experience as a framework for research methodology based on narrative inquiry.

Narrative is an event-driven tool of research. The identification of key events and the details surrounding these is recognised as a significant force in adequately describing the matter under research. Specific events are key determinants in how we recall our life experiences. Our memory of past critical events often leads us to adapt strategies and processes to apply to new situations. Because events are critical parts of people's lives, using them as a main focus for research provides a valuable and insightful tool for getting at the core of what is important in that research. An event-driven approach to research is also a mechanism for dealing with large amounts of data.

Narrative inquiry approaches to human experience and the construction and reconstruction of personal stories blend in such a way that they highlight issues of complexity and human centredness, which are of concern to many researchers. These are recalled in the form of critical events that are instrumental in changing or influencing understanding.

We all have critical events in our lives. Can you recall a story that you have told recently? Was this story constructed around a critical event or experience? Chances are, it was – as is the case, for example, in this short extract from a story by a medical practitioner:

> I tend to think in stories, so let me tell you one. When I was a fourth-year medical student, I had a patient who still sticks in my mind. I was on an internal medicine rotation, and I was nearly finished with medical school. The senior resident had assigned me three or four patients to take primary responsibility for. One was a crinkly, Portuguese-speaking woman in her 70s who, as near as I could tell, had been admitted because – I'll use the technical term here – she didn't feel too good. Her body ached. She felt run-down. She had a cough. She had no fever. Her pulse and blood pressure were fine. But some labs revealed her white count was up. A chest X-ray showed a possible pneumonia – maybe it was, maybe it wasn't. . . . I went to see her twice each day for rounds. . . . To me, she stayed more or less the same. Her heart rate went up. Her heart rate went down. Sometimes she was warm. Sometimes she was cold. We'd give her antibiotics and wait her out, I figured. She'd be fine.
>
> One morning her heart rate was a little up and her skin was a little warm. She had a low-grade fever. 'Keep an eye on her', the senior resident told me. 'Of course', I said, though to me she seemed just as she had been. I made a silent plan to see her in the early afternoon before our usual rounds. But the senior resident went back to check on her twice himself that morning.
>
> It is this little act that I have often thought about since then. It was a small thing, a tiny act of conscientiousness. . . .
>
> The first time he went up, he found she had a high-grade fever. The second time, he transferred her to the intensive care unit. To my great embarrassment and her great fortune, by the time I had a clue about what was going on, he already had her under treatment for what had developed into septic shock from a resistant, fulminant pneumonia.
>
> *(Gawande, 2005, pp. 28–30)*

Stories feature critical events and are the mechanism by which the most important occurrences are transmitted to listeners. In this way critical events are communicated across generations and centuries. People distil those events that are most important. This human ability to distil the most important events in any story is essential to the use of critical events in a method of analysis of narratives.

As we recall experiences, we unfold the story of those experiences. The story, in turn, is associated with a memorable event. That event has carried with it a development of new understanding as a consequence of the particular experience. Perhaps, importantly, it has stood the test of time and retained a place in living memory, where many other details have faded, not to be ever recalled.

The use of a critical event approach to research does not exclude the use of other methods of analysis used in the literature on narrative inquiry. Other methods have tended to treat the stories of human experience in terms based on those used in traditional approaches to narrative, such as literary criticism, and indeed borrow terms of analysis from that approach. We have referred to these in the previous chapters. The basis of these approaches is the use of a storyboard to structure the analysis of narratives.

Connelly and Clandinin (1990) and others offer mechanisms and techniques which can be applied in a narrative research methodology. These mechanisms and techniques, referred to as narrative sketches, describe event, character and structure. Analysis is performed through the scaffold provided by descriptions of the processes, presentation of results, conclusions, risk and negotiation associated with the narratives. These, in turn, are further broken down into a number of subheadings to assist the researcher. It should be noted, however, that while some of these categories are commonly used as general research terms, these authors define them differently within the context of narrative.

It is also appropriate to sound out some warning here to researchers. These approaches rely on a complex series of interrelationships between data sources. The consequent analysis by researchers may result in them drilling into the data so deeply that the essence of a narrative approach is missed – that is, the criticality of an event and its impact on human understanding and action.

This chapter attempts to illuminate the use of critical events to address a number of problems faced by researchers wanting to use a more narrative-based approach, including the vast amount of data and sources a narrative inquiry may generate. It will also address the resulting problem of how to analyse this data without becoming so immersed in it that the critical events, those that shaped and impacted on human understanding, are not missed.

Critical events

What is a critical event?

An event becomes critical when it has the 'right mix of ingredients at the right time and in the right context' (Woods, 1993a, p. 102). A critical event as told in a story reveals a change of understanding or worldview by the storyteller. An event becomes critical if it has some of the following characteristics. It has impacted on the performance of the storyteller in a professional or work-related role. It may have a traumatic component, attract some excessive interest by the public or the media or introduce risk in the form of personal exposure: illness, litigious action or other powerful personal consequence. However, what makes a critical event 'critical' is the impact it has on the storyteller (Bohl, 1995). It is almost always a change experience, and it can only ever be identified afterwards. It is impossible to predict or plan to observe a critical event as might be possible in other research methods. It does need to be noted that an event that is less than critical can still have an impact on a person's performance and functioning.

It is impossible to construct a list of critical events before they occur, as might often be the case in traditional research, in which lists of questions and events are generated prior to the investigation that is of interest to the researcher. It is only in retrospect that an event can be seen to have been critical for the storyteller. The longer the time that passes between the event and recall of the event, the more profound the effect of the event has been and the more warranted is the label *critical* event.

Such events can then be characterised by time, challenge and change. Over time, the mind refines and discards unnecessary detail and retains those elements that have been of changing and lasting value. The critical event will have challenged the storyteller's understanding or worldview. The event is likely to have changed his or her experience and understanding, informing future behaviour and understanding. One note at this point is that later in this chapter, the term *like event* is also used. Although not of the same proportions as a critical event, a like event finds the same or similar events occurring for other people.

Critical events are not necessarily positive. Some critical events are negative in impact. Woods (1993b) describes negative critical events and refers to the use of the term 'counter incidents' by Sikes *et al.* (1985). Mostly in this book, we are concerned with critical events that are positive in their impact on learning. Most researchers take the same viewpoint.

Measor (1985) identifies three types of critical events or 'critical phases': extrinsic, intrinsic and personal. She relates them to the teaching profession; however, they are also applicable to other professions. According to her,

- 'extrinsic' critical events can be produced by historical and political events;
- 'intrinsic' critical events occur within the natural progression of a career. In a teaching career she highlights several critical periods, such as

    1   entering the teaching profession;
    2   first teaching practice;
    3   first 18 months of employment;
    4   three years after taking the first job;
    5   mid-career moves and promotion; and
    6   pre-retirement period.

- 'personal' critical events can be family events, illness and so on.

A critical event is almost always a change experience. This change experience can come about as storytellers encounter some difficulty in integrating their idealised worldview with the reality of their experience. This conflict of belief and experience promotes the development of a critical event as storytellers struggle to accommodate a change to their worldview (Fay, 2000).

A brief background on critical events and human thinking

Discussion of critical events as they occur in human experience and teaching and learning is not new. As Woods (1993b) notes, the significance of critical incidents in people's lives has been highlighted over a significant time frame by many authors, including Strauss (1959), Berger and Kellner (1964), Becker (1966), Walker *et al.* (1976), Measor (1985) and Sparkes (1988). Sikes *et al.* (1985) elaborate the critical events described by these authors as 'highly charged moments and episodes that have enormous consequences for personal change and development' (cited in Woods, 1993b, p. 356). These writings, in combination with French theories of the mid- to late 1960s, have had a major influence on the increasing popularity of narrative in recent decades.

As something of an aside, it is worth noting that critical events are sometimes referred to also as *critical incidents*. Some authors, for instance Woods (1993a, 1993b), even distinguish between these two terms. For him, critical events are largely planned and predicted, whereas critical incidents are unpredicted and unplanned. We do not make such a distinction in this book.

The origin of critical events comes from the area of aviation psychology, and they were first referred to by John Flanagan. During the Second World War, there was a high rate of pilot failure in training, which led Flanagan to developing an analytical method called 'critical incident technique' (CIT). This is a technique in which incidents of success and failure are retrospectively analysed to identify specific behaviours that caused positive or negative outcomes. The first publication in which Flanagan referred to the CIT was *Psychological Bulletin* in 1954. According to him, the CIT is a 'set of procedures for collecting direct observations of human behaviour . . . to facilitate their potential usefulness in solving practical problems and developing broad psychological principles' (Flanagan, 1954, cited in Fountain, 1999, p. 10).

Critical incidents, as Flanagan perceived them, typically included three features: a description of the situation, an account of the actions or behaviour of the key player in the incident and the outcome or result (Fountain, 1999). Flanagan further identified five steps involved in CIT (Byrne, 2001):

1 determining the general aim of the study (i.e. statement of the topic under study);
2 planning and specifying how the actual incidents will be collected;
3 data collection (may be via interviews or observer reports);
4 data analysis (via textual analysis or identification of themes); and
5 interpreting and reporting on the requirements of the incident being studied.

The technique has most frequently been used in organisational psychology, management (particularly human resources management), health care and related instruction.

A timeline of authors who have referred to critical events since Flanagan includes the following:

1954	Flanagan
1959	Strauss
1964	Berger and Kellner
1966	Becker
1967	Glasser and Strauss
1976	Walker
1985	Measor
1985	Benyon
1985	Sikes *et al.*
1988	Sparkes
1990	Strauss and Corbin

The writings by Strauss (and his colleagues) note critical events from a socio-psychoanalytical perspective, focusing on identity. He notes that there is a temporary gap between events and our understanding of them and that the 'world' depends on our interpretation of it. Strauss observed that face-to-face 'interplay' was better envisaged as a story and that, even when interaction is fleeting or occasional, it is likely to have a cumulative, developmental character. Although this is not directly associated with the notion of a critical event, it nonetheless has similar foundations in that it has an impact for change on a human being.

Strauss also suggests that we can be perfectly aware of present action, but we can only make judgements of it when it is already past. Past activities are viewed in a new light through reassessment and selective recollection. The time frame suggested by Strauss is in agreement with that of critical events in that they are deemed critical only in hindsight. And so, their fuller impact on one's understanding and worldview is realised only in retrospect.

The significance of critical events

Critical events are 'critical' because of their impact and profound effect on whoever experiences such an event. They often bring about radical change in the person. These events are unplanned, unanticipated and uncontrolled. To the researcher, the opportunity to 'access' such profound effects holistically is an avenue to making sense of complex and human-centred information.

Woods (1993a) wrote about critical events in relation to teaching and learning. He maintained that they promote understanding in uncommonly accelerated ways and that they are critical for change. Further, critical events seem to have an important preservation and confirmatory function as well as assisting in maintaining a definition of reality and identity against the pressure of contrary forces.

Woods (1993a) deemed critical events to be critical in four ways:

- *They promote student learning in accelerated ways* – for example, through students' attitudes towards learning, understanding of the self, relationships with others, acquisition of knowledge and development of skills. This learning involves a holistic change.
- *They are critical for teacher development* – for example, through pride in their craftsmanship and realisation of the self. (Some argue that the role of a teacher inevitably implies the role of a learner as well.)
- *They restore ideals and commitment in teachers* – critical events maintain a particular definition of reality and identity against the pressure of contrary forces. Critical events permit teachers to retain their ideals despite the assaults that might customarily be made on them. In a sense they may act as a coping strategy.
- *They boost teacher morale* – this can be critical for the profession as a whole.

Woods (1993a) maintained that critical events have a neat and logical kind of symmetry and that there is a distinctive underlying pattern in them, even though, on the surface, this might not be apparent. To go beyond surface appearance requires a methodology that is sensitive to the complexities of human understanding and learning. Discovery of deeper issues requires a more holistic approach that can interface with the chaotic and fuzzy realities of human existence. In the following section we suggest that the use of 'like events' (perhaps this is the way to approach the symmetry that Woods refers to) can be used to provide validity to the event and its analysis by the researcher.

Critical events, like events and other events – categories for analysis of data

> Events are exceptional by virtue of their criticality. This relates not so much to the content (which might be extraordinary), as to the profound effects it has on the people involved.
>
> *(Woods, 1993b, p. 356)*

Collected stories can be categorised into *critical events*, *like events* and *other events*. In doing this, the data is collected from the context of the investigation and analysed to assign events that are 'critical', events that are 'like' and events that are 'other'. The discussion to this point in the chapter has detailed critical events. This section further details the use of like and other events.

An event is classified as a like event if it repeats the context, method and resources used in the critical event but with different people. Like events occur at the same level as the critical event and, because the context is like the critical event, they are labelled 'like events'. For example, in teaching and learning scenarios, they may occur with different students and instructors when the methods and resources are the same. A review of these like events is useful in confirming and/or broadening issues arising from the critical event.

Other anecdotal and incidental information is called 'other events' and may reveal the same issues. These events occur at the same place, context and time as the collected critical and like events. The characteristics of other events might include corridor encounters, lunchtime conversations and the many informal associations which intuitively inform the critical events. The findings of their analysis are interwoven in the analysis of the critical and like events. Table 5.1 summarises definitions of the categories of events discussed so far in this chapter.

For data assigned to the categories of like events or other events, verisimilitude, or the appearance of being true, can be used to ascertain that the story presented in the critical event can be verified. Analyses of like and other events usually highlight similar issues.

Regarding the occurrence of a number of related events (i.e. like events), Gough (1997) perceived narrative's chief advantage as coming from its use in seeing multiple possibilities in real-life experiences. This interconnectedness of events and the view that in the production of meaning every event is related to every other event confirms the use of like events as sources of useful information.

There is no limit to the number of events that might be collected. The categorisation of events into *critical*, *like* and *other* provides a way of approaching the complexity and extent of data that might be collected. A common question in qualitative research is how to manage the amount of data that is collected. The classification of events provides one way of assisting the researcher in this.

Examples of a critical event

Critical events may sometimes have devastating consequences for the future development of individuals' professional careers. Our first story is an observation of such a critical event in an individual's professional life.

TABLE 5.1 Definition of terms *critical*, *like* and *other*

Critical event	An event selected because of its unique, illustrative and confirmatory nature
Like event	Same sequence level as the critical event, further illustrates and confirms and repeats the experience of the critical event
Other event	Further event that takes place at the same time as critical and like events

An air traffic control trainee – a bad day

Walking into the dimly lit 'tower simulator' that replicates an aerodrome control tower at a fictitious airfield I immediately notice the tension and anticipation of two students as they busily prepare for the coming sequence. As in operational airport control towers, one student controller is responsible for Surface Movement Control (SMC) position and one for Tower Control (TWR) position. In the simulator control room two other students take their places as 'pseudo' pilots with an instructor as 'simulator supervisor' seated between them. The simulation supervisor in the control booth commences setting up the scenarios for the planned sequence with a series of initialising commands.

The activity of the students in the simulator is interrupted by the arrival of two instructors scheduled to assess the sequence. Almost immediately the instructors commence the pre-sequence briefing. At some point during this briefing, the simulated visual view of the aerodrome is projected onto the 180° field-of-view screens. Although clearly recognisable as an airfield, there is a discomforting surreal effect, aided in part by the artificially high perspective of the simulated tower and the lack of detailed landforms.

Interrupting the briefing and the final organisation of flight information strips by the SMC and TWR students is a continuous barrage of communication checks between the students and the 'pseudo' pilots in the simulator control booth. On completion of the briefing, one of the instructors in the simulator asks for the sequence to commence with the instruction 'roll'. For the next 60 minutes, the students control various events with the TWR instructor frequently freezing the simulation to make a comment or other instructional intervention.

The sequence did not go well for the TWR student ('George'). . . . A critical event involved a freeze about half-way through and commenced with a barrage of questions directed at the TWR student. These questions were intended to get George to identify the problem. However, they resulted in the instructor, 'Roger', using them as a platform for a longer discourse, at times critical of the student.

Roger: 'The basics aren't happening for you. The aircraft's arrived. The other thing I want you to stop doing is whistling tunes and doing whatever you like while you've got the transmitter selected. . . . We're half an hour into the sequence. You've got a half an hour to prove to me that you've got all the basics there, because it really hasn't happened so far.'

Roger's discourse for the remaining time of the sequence was consistent in his criticism of George, who increasingly appeared stressed and losing confidence in his ability. On completion of the sequence, a debriefing of the students occurred. George was told he failed in the sequence and a short time after was dismissed from the course. I was left wondering if the outcome for George could have been different had the event been more positive, if the instructor had cancelled the sequence and repeated it at another time, or even if George had been rostered with a different instructor on this day. Perhaps the training had been inadequate in its preparation for the dynamic nature of the simulator contrasted to the previous static classroom instruction. Whatever the reason, this event had a life changing impact on the student.

(adapted from Webster, 1998, pp. 138–166)

Critical events in individuals' professional lives may also be related to political events. Our second story relates to a significant political/historical event, which has powerfully impacted on the personal and professional lives of many. This is a story of an academic reflecting on how the event changed his perception of higher education, and perhaps his worldview in general.

A story of an academic

I regard myself belonging to a blessed generation, where the adjective 'blessed' relates to the fact that my life experiences as a citizen of the Czech Republic (and the former Czechoslovakia) are connected to the 'closed' model of governance with a lack of freedom, but also to the free, open, so-called 'post-November' model. I see it as a great advantage that my generation was 'formed' by these two experiences, in other words, that we can compare, and that we are not the 'bearers' of just a single worldview 'paradigm'. To my generation, November 1989 and the key political change-over in Czechoslovakia (the future Czech Republic) brought on by it are associated with a lot of impressions and experiences. In any case it represents an initiating moment similar to some key 'moments' occurring in private lives, because this was an event which has offered us, possibly for the first time, the 'real' open and free (and thus 'uncompromising') space of a significant choice. A choice where nobody had any excuses any more. This was a situation for which a citizen of the communist Czechoslovakia was not in any way prepared, which they were not used to, in which they were not 'competent'. I am not even sure how many of us were then able to (or prepared to) think of the consequences related to this new situation. I am certain that most of us (including this author) rather 'went with the flow' of the current events.

This perception of being 'blessed' equally relates to my experience with the academic environment. To have entered university in 1987 meant to be confronted with an incredibly rigid and enclosed environment, which meant to be 'led by the hand' in the great majority of responsibilities, without being given any choice in anything. It meant only minimal communication with lecturers (the exceptions will forgive me), who, to be on the safe side, preferred the monologic form of lecturing. This was even more apparent in the instance of humanities students like us (in my case history and Russian). Thus, all the more 'vigorous' and 'mischievous' was the life of the actual student community, concentrated mainly in the student halls of residence. Then we perceived the existence of these parallel communities, which are incidentally one of the most significant features of the (post-) totalitarian regimes, as something quite natural.

All the more challenging was the change-over, which was brought on by the events of November 1989. In Czechoslovakia, this change-over was incidentally instigated by university students (or rather a section of them), who played a key role in it. However, it needs to be admitted that the conditions for a real change were fairly limited. And thus we were gaining experience with the open model of academic environments, or even in everyday lives, only very slowly and with a great deal of uncertainty. The fact is that the 'opening up' of universities, in the worldview, disciplinal, methodological and personal sense, meant a 'challenge' and by no means guaranteed a success.

One of the unexpected consequences of the '89 revolution' in Czech universities was the real participation of students in the leading of some (especially humanities and arts-oriented) faculties, or their individual departments and institutes. And this was not in the sense of (future) regular student representation (e.g. by founding the 'senate'), but the more 'revolutionary' representation of students in the university structures. This reflected the unprecedented disorientation and insecurity by which the then university leadership, and obviously the great majority of lecturers, were struck. Some of them were maybe reliving the long-forgotten memories of their own revolutionary engagements of the late 1940s and early 1950s, when Czech universities experienced a wave of communist purges.

I was incidentally such a student representative in the department of Slavonic Studies of a faculty of arts. This meant that we resolutely influenced the structure of studies within individual disciplines, or even of individual subjects. A most prominent pursuit was, for example, the expansion of foreign language teaching, which was very restricted during the communist era. We successfully pushed this through for living languages (particularly English) and even for dead languages. This engagement however rebounded on me two years later, when I was again a 'regular' student, and at the beginning of the academic year was checking my course timetable on a departmental notice board. I stood there with a group of first-years who were doing the same and one of them made a comment: 'Which idiot has come up with so much compulsory Latin?' This came as a bit of a shock to me because the answer was 'Me!' or rather 'We!' Obviously, I did not disclose to those students that this was in fact meant to be a 'bonus' of the 'dearly acquired' freedom. But in that situation I had to admit that November 1989 and my/our conduct then moved me/us to the 'other side of the barricade'.

We often hear clichés about the onset (revival) of academic freedom in Czech universities after 1989, but I think that this incident indicates that the developments of historic events cannot be determined or predicted prior to them. And that most people involved frequently cannot quite find their bearings in them, or even imagine all the possible directions that the further developments may take.

(Jan Holzer, in 'Stories of professional practice', 2005)

Identifying critical events

Critical events are identified through the impact on the storyteller. The level of criticality becomes evident as the story is told. They are unplanned and unanticipated, and they also have the following qualities. They

- exist in a particular context, such as formal organisational structures or communities of practice;

- have an impact on the people involved;
- have life-changing consequences;
- are unplanned;
- may reveal patterns of well-defined stages;
- are only identified after the event; and
- are intensely personal with strong emotional involvement.

The context of the event may exist within an organisational structure and be subject to its governance, discipline processes, authority, operational procedures and performance expectations. Research in human behaviour and organisational change highlights this context.

Critical events occur in a community. Bruner (1986) observed that 'most learning in most settings is a communal activity, a sharing of the culture' (quoted in Woods, 1993b, p. 362). The efficacy of this is well illustrated in critical events, according to Woods (1993a). However, critical events will always contain something that is at the same time outside and beyond structure. Again, Woods (1993a) argued that we all know that this is something special, although exactly why is difficult to explain. Critical events that are of most interest to researchers are most likely to occur within communities of practice. These communities of practice may share values, attitudes and knowledge but, at the same time, may display aspects of these communities that may not always be positive. According to Strauss (1959), groups of every size and composition can force their members in and out of all kinds of temporary identities – what he refers to as 'status-forcing'. Further, Strauss (1959) noted that even when interaction is fleeting, or occasional, it is likely to have a cumulative, developmental character. In relation to this, Strauss referred to Erikson (1956), who pointed out that a sense of identity 'is never gained nor maintained once and for all. Like a good conscience, it is constantly lost and regained' (quoted in Strauss, 1959, p. 109).

In investigating critical events, the researcher's involvement in a community of practice and identifying features of these critical events will also provide useful like and other events to further support research findings.

Criticality relates not so much to the content (which might be extraordinary) as to the profound effects it has on the people involved. The significance of critical incidents in people's lives has been noted by Strauss (1959), Becker (1966), Measor (1985) and Sparkes (1988). The student undergoing a final assessment in which unsatisfactory performance will result in suspension from the course and possible loss of a career (as indicated earlier in the story of the air traffic trainee) is one example. Critical events lie between the flashpoint incidents and the long-term consequences.

Writing about teacher education, Woods (1993a) declared critical events to be

unplanned, unanticipated and uncontrolled. They are flash-points that illuminate in an electrifying instant some key problematic aspect of the teacher's role and which contain, in the same instant, the solution. The dramatising of the incident elevates the teacher-pupil interaction to a new level and ensures that it is imbued with a new meaning on a permanent basis. There might be a higher proportion of such incidents during critical periods, such as one's initiation into teaching.

(Woods, 1993a, p. 357)

Some argued that critical events have a structure that presents well-defined stages. Woods (1993a) suggested the following stages:

1   *Conceptualisation* – the process is set in motion by an initial spark or moment of conception.
2   *Preparation and planning* – this involves briefing, resourcing and enskilling; objectives are clarified and plans made.
3   *Divergence* – an 'explosion' stage in which students are encouraged to be innovative and creative, explore opportunities and stretch their abilities. New and completely unforeseen teaching and learning opportunities arise.
4   *Convergence* – an integrating stage in which products of the previous stage are examined to find those that best serve the aims of the enterprise.
5   *Consolidation* – work is refined in the writing up, editing, picture-mounting, performance or whatever medium or means of expression is being used.
6   *Celebration* – clear signalling of the end of the event.

However, to assert that critical events take on such a structure does not appear to take into account the fact that critical events by their nature often involve clearly chaotic activity and considerable problems for coordination. This makes imposing a structural view of their development problematic. It is important to maintain the core awareness that critical events are unplanned and unanticipated. Their identification occurs through capturing and reflecting on events and confirmatory stories (through 'like' and 'other' events) by the researcher. It is this unplanned and unanticipated character of critical events that supports the use of a narrative inquiry research approach to uncover and reveal those issues that are often not reported through more traditional research methods.

Collecting stories

In exploring critical events, the researcher engages in the storytelling. One way this is achieved is through the use of open-ended questions, whereby the researcher invites the research participants to engage in storytelling.

Strauss and Corbin (1998) noted the following:

> Descriptive details chosen by a storyteller usually are consciously or unconsciously selective, based on what he or she saw or heard or thought to be important. Although description often is meant to convey believability and to portray images, it also is designed to persuade, convince, express, or arouse passions.

(p. 18)

According to Strauss and Corbin (1998), asking good questions will enhance development of the evolving theory. They divided these questions into the following groups:

1   *Sensitising* questions – What is going on here (issues, problems, concerns)? Who are the actors involved? How do they define the situation? What is its meaning to them?
2   *Theoretical* questions – What is the relationship of one concept to another (how do they compare or relate)? How do events and actions change over time?
3   *Practical* and *structural* questions – Which concepts are well developed and which are not? What, when and how is data gathered for an evolving theory? Is the developing theory logical?

Reighart and Loadman (1984) detailed how they developed a system for analysing the content of students' narrative reports of critical/significant events that occur during experiences in two introductory teacher education courses. Their content analysis system was a hierarchical classification in which each event was classified in four ways:

1   *type of experience* (i.e. instructional strategy in which the event occurs);
2   *type of event* (i.e. teacher responsibility or area of teacher decision making);
3   *category of event* (i.e. specific situation or behaviour during an event); and
4   *affect of event* (i.e. feelings expressed about the event).

Further, they identified the major processes involved in developing the content analysis system as the following:

1   development of an initial set of categories based on students' reports of events;
2   trial analysis of critical events using the initial categories and subsequent revision of the category system;
3   development of rater skill and determination of inter-rater reliability;
4   establishment of procedures to be used in classifying events; and
5   content analysis of a large sample of critical events.

In a narrative inquiry, questions should be structured in such a way that they encourage reflection and recall of the critical event. Time and experience are critical here, as narrative is essentially temporal. By allowing time and experience to work their way into the inquiry and by the creation of situations of trust, stories are told that reflect the participant's experience and understanding (Webster, 1998).

The following questions are some that we have found useful in getting participants to reflect on events of the past that have had influence on them. It is useful for the researcher to commence by establishing the time frame and location of the event being investigated:

1   Think of one memory you have of <context of investigations>. Tell me about it.
2   Thinking back to <context of investigation> what do you remember or recall?
3   If there was one main memory of <context of investigation> what would it be?
4   Within the <context of investigation> do you remember a particularly stressful period?
5   How would you say has it influenced you?
6   What role did others play in this event (critical others)?
7   If there was one thing you would say about, that event it would be . . .
8   How would you describe or tell of the changing influence and long-lasting effects?

Informal contacts and opportunities provide research data as well as formal opportunities. While questions serve the researcher well, listening carefully to stories from the wide range of contexts in which people tell their stories (i.e. being a good listener) provides the researcher with much valuable data and will reveal in its own way the critical events of those involved. Further questions might then be designed and used to elaborate or clarify aspects of the stories that have already been told.

Analysing and reporting critical events

Often a collection of personal stories of experience is not easily summarised or condensed into data tables, as survey results can be. Rather, responding to the need for a context for readers, a sense of the entire inquiry is useful. A narrative sketch as applied to critical events is one way to achieve this end. Connelly and Clandinin (1990) described narrative sketches as reproduced here:

> Like the notes playgoers receive as they are escorted to their seats, it has broad descriptions of scene and plot and a number of sub-sketches of key characters, spaces and major events.
>
> *(p. 11)*

These sketches are shaped by those records that are most telling, that is to say critical events. Just as a story recounts the most memorable and impressionable events, these critical events reflect the most memorable and impressionable stories. (Note that Connelly and Clandinin and many other authors in the field of narrative research used the terms *scene* and *plot*. We prefer to use the terms *place* and *event*, as they have more general meaning and wider application.)

The quality of the narrative sketch is influenced by two criteria, 'broadening' and 'burrowing', according to Connelly and Clandinin (1990). 'Broadening' occurs through generalisation and is of lesser value in a narrative sketch, whereas 'burrowing' places emphasis on the actual event. In 'burrowing' the focus is on the qualities of the event, that is, reflecting on the meaning of the event in terms of the present and future considerations. 'Burrowing' into interviews and other data sources is the method of analysis used in this book to identify human-centred research issues and inform the development of prototypes. Thus, as Connelly and Clandinin (1990) and McEwan and Egan (1995) suggested, the highlighted stories are those that exemplify the nature of the complexity and human centredness of an event, as seen through the eyes of the researcher in collaboration with the people involved in those stories.

Summary

Connelly and Clandinin (1990) suggested that narrative operating in educational inquiry generates a new agenda of theory-practice relations. These are operationalised through two agendas. The first is to let time and experience work their way in the inquiry. The second is the collaborative nature of the storytelling, incorporating both participant and researcher stories. Both of these considerations are integral to the methodology used in this book.

Time and experience are critical, as narrative is essentially temporal. By allowing time and experience to work their way into the inquiry through telling and listening to stories and the creation of situations of trust, stories are told that enable narratives to reflect the experience and understanding of learning. These approaches need to be gentle because of what is at stake. Eisner (1988) described the difference of this approach by contrasting the collaboration in the research environment to that of the 'commando raid conduct' of more traditional empirical approaches.

Merely listening, recording and fostering participant stories while ignoring the researcher's stories is both impossible and unsatisfying. Connelly and Clandinin (1990) pointed out that researchers need to tell their stories, too. In the telling of researcher stories, the stories of the participants merge with the researcher's to form new stories that are collaborative in nature. These become the collaborative document that is written on the research, which opens new possibilities for further research.

6

RETHINKING VALIDITY
AND RELIABILITY

Introduction

There is a consensus in the literature on narrative research that it should not be judged by the same criteria as those that are applied to more traditional and broadly accepted qualitative and quantitative research methods. (See, for instance, Polkinghorne (1988), Riessman (1993), Huberman (1995), Amsterdam and Bruner (2000) and Geelan (2003).) Traditional approaches to research tend to be based on scientific methods, facts and processes. Narrative inquiry and storytelling research, as defined in the other chapters in this book, seek to elaborate and investigate individual interpretations and worldviews of complex and human-centred events. It is more concerned with individual truths than identifying generalisable and repeatable events. We see narrative as a unique, holistic research method that redefines measures that are used to rate and compare research. Therefore, at the very least, the definitions of reliability and validity, commonly used in traditional research, require a rethinking and redefining for narrative research. This chapter seeks to do that.

To state matters succinctly, reliability in narrative research usually refers to the dependability of the data, while validity typically refers to the strength of the analysis of data, the trustworthiness of the data and ease of access to that data (Polkinghorne, 1988). As noted by Riessman (1993), concepts of verification and procedures for establishing validity (from the experimental model) rely on measurable and objectivist assumptions that are largely irrelevant to narrative studies. A personal narrative is not meant to be read as an exact record of what happened, nor is it a mirror of the world 'out there'. This can be, of course, an upsetting view to those researchers who may be troubled by anything that does not neatly conform to the divides of traditional quantitative and qualitative views of research methods.

Polkinghorne (1988) and Huberman (1995) provided, in our view, some of the more helpful insights for researchers contemplating a storytelling approach to their research. Polkinghorne (1988) argues that the validity of narrative is more closely associated with meaningful analysis than with consequences. He also maintains that reliability is not stability of measurement but rather trustworthiness of the notes or transcripts. According to Polkinghorne, we need to re-orientate our measures in using narrative. It is not satisfactory to apply the previous criteria of more traditional approaches, that is to say the measures of validity and reliability, to narrative. Rather, what is sought are new measures such as access, honesty, verisimilitude, authenticity, familiarity, transferability and economy (Huberman, 1995).

This view is a departure from an objectivist definition of research validity and reliability. Instead, access to reliable and trustworthy records of the stories as told by individuals is the cornerstone of validity and reliability. This leads to demands being made of the narrative researcher to collect, record and make accessible the data in ways that can be understood and used by those analysing, auditing or having an interest in reading the data. Given this departure from traditional views of what constitutes validity and reliability, researchers intending to use a narrative approach will need to detail how they address validity and reliability. The remainder of this chapter attempts to outline a framework of criteria by which this can be done.

Established ways of viewing validity and reliability

Validity

The concept of *validity* has largely been narrowed down by formal science as referring to tests or measuring instruments that aim to produce certainty. Statistical results are often interpreted to mean that the finding is important, without considering whether the research method is appropriate to the matter being researched. In narrative research a finding is significant if it is important (Polkinghorne, 1988). Narrative research does not produce conclusions of certainty. In narrative-based research, validity is more concerned with the research being well grounded and supportable by the data that has been collected. It does not provide results that produce generalisable truths, 'prescribing' how things are or ought to be.

By retaining an emphasis on the linguistic reality of human experience, narrative research is not limited by formal systems and their particular type of rigour. The results of narrative research cannot claim to correspond exactly to what has actually occurred. In that sense, we cannot claim that narrative research results are 'true', if 'truth' is taken to mean exact correspondence to reality. As Karl Popper pointed out, we cannot demonstrate the 'truth' of statements; we can at best demonstrate their falsity (Polkinghorne, 1988).

Prevailing concepts of verification and procedures for establishing validity (from the experimental model) pertain to realist assumptions and consequently are largely irrelevant to narrative studies. A personal narrative is not meant to be read as an exact record of what happened, nor is it a mirror of the world 'out there'. Our readings of data are themselves located in particular discourses (Riessman, 1993). Narrative does not strive for 'validity in representing something "out there" in the world, or even in expressing one's logically reasoned notions of how things "out there" ought to work' (Amsterdam and Bruner, 2000, pp. 13–14).

Approaches commonly applied to qualitative data may not suit narrative inquiry. Triangulation, for instance, is a tool that qualitative researchers use to satisfy the validity of their research. It is a common approach in qualitative research for claiming validity, and it involves using a variety of data sources, the outcomes of which point to the same conclusions. However, it is not necessarily applicable to storytelling-based research. Indeed, triangulation in a storytelling sense is almost impossible to achieve, and it is our view that a framework of *critical* events, *like* events and *other* events is more applicable (see Chapter 5). The storytelling approach to research cannot adopt mechanisms that have found acceptance in other research paradigms without questioning their suitability and applicability to the context of the research and their sensitivity to the individual's understanding of the events that surround and involve him or her.

Silverman (2000) perceived the use of triangulation by qualitative researchers as a means of convincing themselves and their audience that

> [b]y having cumulative view of data drawn from different contexts, we may . . . be able to triangulate the 'true' state of affairs by examining where the different data intersect. In this way, some qualitative researchers believe that triangulation may improve the reliability of a single method.
>
> *(p. 121)*

The use of different methods to create a triangulation that 'pinpoints' the 'real' state of affairs is one approach used to address issues of validity. Cohen *et al.* (2000) regarded triangulation techniques as an 'attempt to map out, or explain more fully, the richness and complexity of human behaviour by studying it from more than one standpoint' (p. 112).

At first, this argument would seem reasonable – that multiple confirmatory sources of data ensure a level of validity because findings are less likely to be able to be 'constructed' or influenced by the research techniques or by the researchers themselves. However, if one subscribes to the view that the 'real' picture is context bound, that is to say the same set of interactions would have a different meaning in different contexts, there is a fundamental difficulty in trying to bring together data collected in different contexts to make overall sense of a phenomenon. Practical issues arise with using multiple data sets in an attempt to triangulate. For example, what happens when different techniques provide results that do not corroborate each other? The researcher may be compelled to either discard one set or 'force' some agreement through his or her analysis.

A number of authors have expressed their reservations about the merit of triangulation.

For instance, Silverman (2000) pointed out that 'it is usually far better to celebrate the partiality of your data and delight in the particular phenomena that it allows you to inspect' (p. 112). For Flick (1998), triangulation 'is not a tool or a strategy of validation, but an alternative to validation' (p. 230). Richardson (2001) went further in disputing the concept of triangulation, utilising the metaphor of a crystal that appears different depending on the position of the viewer.

By using triangulation, researchers are in a sense searching for the one, ultimate truth. However, as a number of authors, including Lather (1993), have indicated, there is no 'single' truth but rather a multiplicity of truths.

> Truth is multiple, partial, endlessly deferred validities which construct a site of development for a validity of transgression that runs counter to the standard validity of correspondence: a non-referential validity interested in how discourse does its work, where transgression is defined as the game of limits . . . at the border of disciplines.
>
> *(p. 675)*

Perhaps most important about this argument is that multiple interpretations are valid, that the real test of the validity of any research should ultimately be done by those who read it and that they should be the ones to decide on whether an account is 'believable'.

Some authors argue that qualitative research (especially unstructured narrative interviews) tends to score higher on the matter of validity than quantitative approaches but lower on reliability (e.g. Mishler, 1990). Ganzevoort (2005) maintained that this may also depend on the quality of data collection. Ganzevoort further pointed out that, on the other hand, reliability, the probability that replication will yield similar results, may not be as easy to achieve in narrative research. However, Huberman (1995) contended that if the narrative researcher can demonstrate rigorous methods of reading and interpreting that would enable other researchers to track down his or her conclusions, then reliability, in terms of access and honesty, can be achieved.

Reliability

In quantitative research, *reliability* refers to the consistency and stability of measuring instruments. In narrative research, reliability usually refers to the dependability of the data. Reliability is achieved not by the stability of measurement but rather the 'trustworthiness' of the notes or transcripts (Polkinghorne, 1988).

The capacity of instruments to return similar or same results when applied to different samples is a valued outcome in the empirical/scientific research model. However, for narrative, it can be neither expected nor assumed that the outcomes from one narrative or a collection of stories will consistently return the same views or outcomes. With narrative's emphasis on individual human experience of reality and the impact of critical events on our understanding, the differences between individuals are to be expected, indeed valued. This highlights a fundamental difference in our view. Reliability from an empirical point of view is concerned with a result that is applicable across samples, whereas reliability for narrative relates to the experience of individuals. Instead of reporting results of statistical measures, narrative reports events of human experience. The reliability is not the statistical measure; rather, it is measured by the accuracy and accessibility of the data, so that any reader can get hold of the relevant text or transcript.

In addition, there are aspects of reliability that are closely associated with narrative, such as persuasiveness and coherence of the data. As Riessman (1993) suggested, persuasiveness is greatest when theoretical claims are supported with evidence from informants' accounts and when alternative interpretations of the data are considered. Agar and Hobbs (1982) proposed three kinds of narrative coherence: global, local and themal. They point out that in narrative, coherence must be as 'thick' as possible, ideally relating to all the three levels. Investigators must continuously modify initial hypotheses about speakers' beliefs and goals (global coherence) in light of the structure of particular narratives (local coherence) and recurrent themes that unify the text (themal coherence).

Rethinking validity and reliability

Rethinking validity and reliability is the focus of the remainder of this chapter, and it is based on concepts proposed by Polkinghorne, Clandinin and Connelly, Huberman and others. We have found these concepts the most useful for the purposes of constructing a more narrative-orientated framework of validity and reliability.

According to Polkinghorne (1988), we need to re-orientate our measures in using narrative. It is not satisfactory to apply traditional criteria of validity and reliability to narrative. Rather, it appears beneficial to look for new measures, such as access, honesty, verisimilitude, authenticity, familiarity, transferability and economy (Huberman, 1995).

Access

Access can be viewed in two ways. First, there is the access by readers of the study to the participants, their cultural context and the process of construction of knowledge between the researcher and participants of the study. The second means of access is the availability and the representation to the same audience of the research notes, transcripts and data on which the researcher has based the findings (see also the section on data coding later in this chapter).

Access to context, process and construction of knowledge

When considering the frameworks and shaping processes impacting on a narrative study, we refer to the model suggested by Connelly and Clandinin, which might be summarised as processes of *negotiation, structures (time, place and events), tools, conclusions and risks.* This model is further referred to in Chapter 9.

Although some of these categories are commonly used as general research terms, these terms are defined differently within the context of narrative. Processes provide a starting point by setting the scene and the context of the study. *Negotiation* describes the pathway of communication between the research, the characters and the contexts in which the study is set. The *structure* provides a means of making sense of *time, place and events*. The tools are those that allow for documenting the aspects of complexity and human centredness. For narrative inquiry, undertaken, for instance, by a university researcher (or a team of researchers), the negotiation of entry into the research environment begins with the gaining of permissions, such as the acquisition of ethical approval from a university committee on ethics in human research (or an equivalent body), the organisation in which the research is to be undertaken, and the individual participants. Other dimensions of this negotiation process for the study might also involve development of effective working relationships with others in the research setting that facilitate access to information, resources, documentation and access to facilities.

As a part of negotiation, the rights and responsibilities of the researcher and participants need to be considered. Therefore, negotiations with regard to ethical issues within the study are not only concerned with the formal application for confirmation of the study by a university or research institution but, perhaps more importantly, are reflected in the procedures used in the conduct of the study.

The components of *structure* (*time, place and events*) create a framework typically applied to literary analyses (often these are referred to as time, scene and plot); however, they are also applied in narrative inquiry. Time, place and events provide the structure to view the processes that inform issues of complexity in the research story. This framework helps create the experiential quality of the narrative study.

Time is essential to explaining the *events*. A basic explanatory event or plot structure contains a beginning, middle and end, which in varying ways relate to past, present and future (Connelly and Clandinin, 1990). Data sources are then attached to each of these temporal categories. Carr (1986) associated time-related structures to dimensions of human experience, including significance, intention and value. An example of how time-related structures can be represented diagrammatically is provided in Figure 6.1.

The *place* (scene) is a descriptive account of the setting of the research and might include both description and diagrams of the scene (buildings, room layout or equipment). There may be the need to include some comment on 'behind the scenes' events, as often the functioning of a scene is reliant on a number of supports and infrastructures. However, it would appear that, before any of the processes can be understood, the scene needs to be set. Any research report has to provide its readers with an exploration or a description of the scene from which the narrative is drawn. Welty (1979) described time and place as essential to narrative and 'as informing as an old gossip' (p. 163).

The unfolding of *events* (plot) is described in relation to the data collected and the processes undertaken in the conduct of the study. Other aspects of the events can describe the context of the study, the literature, the research questions and the interrelationship between all of these aspects.

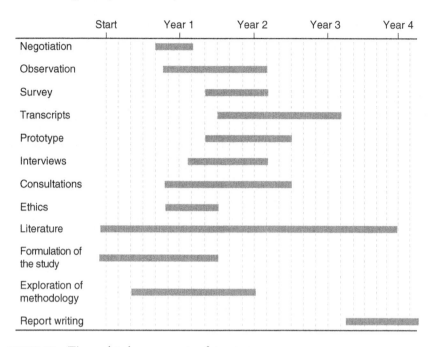

FIGURE 6.1 Time-related components of structure

Narrative inquiry may require a mix of tools and data collection techniques, such as observation, surveys, documentation (including letters, curricula and policies), interviews and transcripts. In some instances, a further tool might be used to assist the findings of the research and include, for example, some prototype materials or resources. Discussion of the tools and collection techniques and schedules provides a framework for the data analysis. This discussion sets the logic behind the record keeping of the collected data and is instrumental to any reader's understanding of how to trace any specific parts of the data collected.

In establishing the integrity of the methodology of narrative inquiry, the benefits of narrative cannot be viewed without due consideration of the risks involved. *Intersubjectivity*, *smoothing* and other constraints are dangers and potential abuses of the narrative inquiry method, according to Connelly and Clandinin (1990). *Intersubjectivity* is the easy slipping into a commitment to the whole narrative plot, and the researcher's role in it, and losing sight of the various fine lines that this approach treads (this risk can be minimised through the use of the *critical* event, *like* event and *other* event technique). *Smoothing* is the tendency to invoke a positive result regardless of the indications of the data. Other limitations may be imposed by the constraints of the culture, sensitivities of the discussions the researcher becomes engaged in, scheduling and the operational context of the study.

Although all of the aforementioned points are noted as constraints and possible limitations, it should also be acknowledged that in the narrative inquiry methodology, they are equally seen as integral to the story. Thus, whereas they might be constraints from the traditional research perspective, within the context of the narrative, they may be merely further characteristics of the scene, the plot or the make-up of the characters.

Access to data

When employing the critical event narrative inquiry model (as described in the previous chapter), it is important to provide the reader with access to the research data, so that the reader can easily trace the data back. Based on the use of a structure of events, we have found the following way of coding the data to provide ease of access and to further support the researcher's analysis. Our simple approach uses a number of volumes to contain the transcripts of narratives collected by the researcher. As each event is recorded and transcribed, each event and also each episode within the event are given a unique identifier. For each volume containing episodes of data collection, the event and episode are given identifying tags, and the data (usually in the form of transcripts) is page numbered and line numbered. The core requirement of any codifying system is that it enables data at all levels to be tracked to its source.

For example, an event named 'student experience' is tagged 'SX', an episode named 'year level and subject' is tagged 'yls' and a transcript of stories of experience by a student is then identified by a coded name and date-tagged as 'cnd'. A referencing system can be built up to quote within a research report that would allow any reader to visit the record of data of the event being described. In our hypothetical example here, a quote from the transcript might look like SX:yls/cnd: Page/line reference. An example of this system is as follows:

30 'This is an example of the coding system used in our own research'
Sample1:2006/courseX/Pat: 9/30

Another example might be a URL from a deep-level website, which provides a model of a pathway that leads to a specific line of information on a specific page, such as

www.university.edu/medicine/units/pdmp/med234/module1/time. html#s3

Honesty, verisimilitude and authenticity

Honesty

Guba and Lincoln (1981), in their exploration of the human as a research 'instrument' in what they call naturalistic inquiry, highlighted the following characteristics that support a claim of trustworthiness of narrative research. These included the following:

1   *Responsiveness* – humans as 'instruments' can sense and respond to all personal and environmental cues that exist, and, by virtue of this responsiveness, they can interact with the situation, sense its dimensions and make them explicit.
2   *Adaptability* – humans (as imperfect as they are) are virtually infinitely adaptable; they can collect information about multiple factors simultaneously at multiple levels.

3 *Holistic emphasis* – only humans are capable of grasping the complexity of a phenomenon and its surroundings in their entirety.

4 *Knowledge base expansion* – humans are capable of working simultaneously in the domains of propositional and tacit knowledge; expanding the propositional to the realm of tacit, unexplained, subconscious will create depth and richness of understanding of social and organisational settings.

5 *Procedural immediacy* – humans are able to process data just as soon as these become available and generate hypotheses on the spot.

6 *Opportunities for clarification and summarisation* – humans are capable of summarising data on the spot and 'feeding' it back to the respondents for clarification and correction.

7 *Opportunity to explore atypical or idiosyncratic responses* – humans can explore responses not only to test their validity but also to achieve a higher level of understanding.

The trustworthiness of the human instrument is assessable in much the same way as is trustworthiness of any 'paper-and-pencil instrument'. A human instrument is capable of refinement in the same way as any other research instrument. There is no reason to believe that humans cannot approach a level of trustworthiness similar to that claimed for ordinary standardised tests. In addition, both facts and interpretations for a case report must be subjected to scrutiny by respondents who earlier acted as sources for that information. Thus, negotiation is essential if the criteria of trustworthiness are to be met adequately (Guba and Lincoln, 1981).

Another recommendation by Guba and Lincoln (1981) is the use of a set of questions that can be used as a checklist for researchers to assess the trustworthiness of their research. In adapting their questions, researchers might ask about the following:

• *Truth value* – How can one establish confidence in the 'truth' of the findings?
• *Applicability* – How can one determine the extent to which the findings of the inquiry are applicable elsewhere?
• *Consistency* – Are there any patterns emerging?
• *Neutrality* – Are conditions of an inquiry not influenced by the biases, motivations or interests of the inquirer?

Lincoln and Guba (1985) summarised the issue of trustworthiness in qualitative research by declaring as follows:

> to demonstrate 'truth value', the researcher must show that he or she has *represented those multiple constructions adequately*, that is, that the *constructions . . . that have been arrived at via the inquiry are credible to the constructors of the original multiple realities*.
>
> (Lincoln and Guba, 1985, p. 296)

Thus, the trustworthiness of the narrative research lies in the confirmation by the participants of their reported stories of experience.

Verisimilitude or truthfulness

There are three aspects of *verisimilitude* that the narrative researcher may find helpful in his or her research. First, the research and reporting of stories and their critical events should resonate with the experience of the researcher. Second, the reporting should appear to have a level of plausibility. And third, when using a critical events approach, the truthfulness of accounts and reporting results will be confirmed through like and other events.

The reader experience resonating with the experience of the researcher is a significant aspect of narrative inquiry. The story sounds true because either it reminds the reader about something that has happened to him or her or it opens a new window to the reader. Sometimes this may generate new understandings by the reader, whereby, upon reading a story, the reader gains a new understanding of an experience.

Plausibility is the sense that what is reported is in fact realistic and that it is not subject to constraints and risks, such as, for instance, the 'Hollywood effect' and other risks associated with narrative inquiry (as explained in Chapter 2).

In using a critical events model, the identification of *like* and *other* events will assist claims of verisimilitude. *Like* events, by their very nature, will record similar experiences and act as a confirming source of *critical* events. The use of like and other events is reported in detail in the preceding chapter.

In conclusion, Bruner made the following insightful comment on verisimilitude:

> Unlike the constructions generated by logical and scientific procedures that can be weeded out by falsification, narrative constructions can only achieve 'verisimilitude'. Narratives, then, are a version of reality whose acceptability is governed by convention and 'narrative necessity' rather than by empirical verification and logical requiredness, although ironically we have no compunction about calling stories true or false.
>
> *(Bruner, 1991, pp. 4–5)*

Another concept that is often used when evaluating narrative research is *authenticity*, and it is intertwined with the concept of verisimilitude. Authenticity can perhaps be most powerfully achieved when the researcher provides enough information in order to convince the reader that the story is told in a serious and honest way. The sense of authenticity of a story may be, for instance, achieved through sufficient narrative coherence.

Woods (1993b) highlighted the role of critical others (e.g. experts in a particular field of learning) in contributing to the authenticity of teachers' work. These critical others, he argues, provide verisimilitude to teachers' work by contributing to the integrity of knowledge both within itself and with the learner's self. This integrity is, according to Woods, encouraged by and reflected 'in the holism of space, time and personnel; by providing and fostering information and communication skills; and by validating teachers' and pupils' work within the particular discipline' (Woods, 1993b, p. 368).

Familiarity

Amsterdam and Bruner (2000) referred to *familiarity* as 'dulling' in that 'when our ways of conceiving of things become routine, they disappear from consciousness and we cease to know *that* we are thinking in a certain way or *why* we are doing so' (p. 1). They further declare that 'familiarity insulates habitual ways of thinking from inspections that might find them senseless, needless, and unserviceable' (p. 2). They point out the importance of 'interpersonal distancing to make the familiar strange again, to rescue the taken-for-granted and bring it back into mind' (p. 1). Bruner borrows the concept of making 'the familiar strange again' from the Russian formalists, as he further refers to it in his 2002 publication *Making Stories: Law, Literature, Life.*

Besides acknowledging the impact and influence of familiarity, it is important to realise and accept that things do not stay constantly the same. This aspect of familiarity/unfamiliarity plays quite a significant role in stories, as Bruner (2002) suggested:

> For there to be a story, something unforeseen must happen. Story is enormously sensitive to whatever challenges our conception of the canonical. It is an instrument not so much for solving problems as for finding them. . . . We more often tell stories to forewarn than to instruct.
>
> *(p. 12)*

In that respect it can be argued that critical events themselves capture that 'unforeseen', and this in itself has the capacity to provide a perspective that makes the 'familiar strange'. This has further significance for reflection on practice, in that it enables us to look at particular professional practices not only as established and characteristic of a particular field but also as a way of thinking, 'a way of life' (Amsterdam and Bruner, 2000, p. 282).

Bruner (2002) perceived two motives for looking at narrative through the notion of familiarity:

> One is to control it or sanitize its effects – as in law, where tradition forges procedures for keeping the stories of plaintiffs and defendants within recognized bounds . . . or as in psychiatry, where patients must be helped to tell the right kinds of stories in order to get well. The other motive for studying narrative is to understand it so as to cultivate its illusions of reality, to 'subjectivize' the self-evident declaratives of everyday life.
>
> *(p. 11)*

Transferability

Lincoln and Guba (1985) suggested *transferability* as an 'analog to external validity'. Transferability in narrative inquiry thus implies that the researcher provides a sufficient base to permit a person contemplating application in another setting to make the needed comparisons of similarity.

Transferability in the critical event narrative inquiry proposed in this book is primarily provided by the use of critical, like and other events. In our view, the critical, like and other events described in the context of a narrative inquiry provide such richness of detail and accessibility that a reader should be able to make applications in another setting.

Some studies, in fact, attempt to demonstrate the transferability of findings. One such attempt took the outcomes of critical events and used these to guide the development of a training programme. For further details on this, see Nadler (1982).

Economy

Economy is an aspect of critical event narrative inquiry that will be of substantial benefit to the researcher. Narratives can be very deep, and the research will often contain large amounts of data. The mechanisms for analysing these large amounts of data are challenging and confronting to the researcher. With transcripts perhaps running to many volumes of collected data, an efficient and economical approach is required that will not compromise the integrity of the data or its findings. Some of the tools to assist analysis of narratives can lead the researcher to seemingly endless categorisation of data, with difficulty in determining an end point. The identification and use of critical events, on the other hand, provide both a means of transfer-ability and indicators of important issues and outcomes of the research.

Ethical issues

Added to the range of aspects and concepts related to validity and reliability in narrative research are associated ethical issues, which should always be considered when undertaking any data analysis. Because the nature of qualitative research typically requires observation and interaction with groups, it is thus expected that certain ethical issues may arise. Miles and Huberman (1994) listed several issues that researchers should consider when analysing data. They cautioned researchers to be aware of these and other issues before, during and after conduct of research. Some issues involved the following:

- informed consent (do participants have full knowledge of what is involved?);
- harm and risk (can the study hurt participants?);
- honesty and trust (is the researcher being truthful in presenting data?);

- privacy, confidentiality and anonymity (will the study intrude too much into group behaviours?); and
- intervention and advocacy (what should researchers do if participants display harmful or illegal behaviour?).

Summary

Narrative offers many appealing features to researchers seeking a human-centred approach. Its supporters argue that it provides insight to those human traits of understanding that may be neglected in traditional and modernist approaches to research. There is a belief amongst educational researchers that the contribution of narrative is our understanding of ourselves and the complex nature of our humanity (McEwan and Egan, 1995). However, in using narrative inquiry for research, it behoves the researcher to define the ways of viewing that research; traditional meanings need to be redefined in terms of newer ways of viewing, using measures of access, honesty, verisimilitude, authenticity, familiarity, transferability and economy.

7

NARRATIVE INQUIRY AS A RESEARCH METHOD AND QUALITY OF LEARNING AND TEACHING IN HIGHER EDUCATION

Introduction

While the previous chapter discussed the issues of validity and reliability in the context of narrative inquiry, this chapter introduces the concepts of quality assurance and control in higher education as complex and human-centred phenomena which have been embraced by higher education world over. The authors argue that narrative inquiry is well suited as both a research method enabling investigation of these phenomena in higher education globally and as an alternative evaluation method enabling higher education institutions to unpack complex issues related to quality which are currently hard to investigate in depth using largely surveys and statistical methods.

Quality assurance and control in higher education as concepts have been embraced by higher education institutions globally. Driven by the need for governments to substantiate the spending of public funding, evidence has been sought that such monies are being well spent. To satisfy bureaucrats, institutions have been required to present evidence in a standardised quantitative form.

Early critics of the approach voiced the concern that such approaches failed to address real issues of quality associated with learning and teaching in higher education. This criticism remains with some leading academics recently acknowledging that new approaches must be adopted to provide data that will inform future decision making.

Attempting to provide evidence of quality in learning and teaching introduces the complexities of human endeavours such as learning. Regardless, institutions seek survey data and other metrics in an attempt to provide required quantitative evidence. It is the experience of the authors that current approaches adopted broadly by higher education institutions and agencies are quantitative and survey based.

Over the past decade higher education – particularly in Australia – has seen an increase in private providers. These institutions often have smaller populations of students compared to larger public government-funded institutions.

This chapter explores what a narrative approach to quality in higher education may present to those institutions with small student cohorts seeking data on quality in their learning and teaching. At the same time this chapter suggests a research approach that may be useful to those interested in investigating quality in the small cohort of students engaged in learning and teaching within the context of higher education.

The chapter concludes by suggesting a research approach to those interested in investigating higher education quality in the private higher education context or small cohorts of students.

Factors and issues associated with quality in higher education that align with narrative inquiry

Research on quality in higher education has relied on a variety of approaches, mostly quantitative, with fewer being based on approaches that may reveal issues or considerations not easily suited to being identified by more traditional quantitative based methodologies.

There are factors associated with quality assurance research that appear to align with the rationale for adopting a narrative approach. The factors discussed in this chapter include the following:

- Sample size;
- Broad adoption of quantitative research approaches; and
- Identifying critical issues associated with the complexity of learning.

Sample size

In smaller private higher education institutions (in Australia the number of private higher education institutions is almost three times the number of universities), the availability of sample size suitable for quantitative approaches is restricted. Within Australia a large number of private institutions have less than a thousand students often spread across multiple awards and a collection of subjects. Obtaining a high response rate across a large sample of students is a challenge faced by private providers, resulting in too few responses or sample size for a valid or reliable analysis. It can be argued that the exercise becomes one of attempting to satisfy a regulatory environment rather than obtaining valid results that will inform changes resulting in improvement.

Type of evaluation methods

In an era of surveys, across a wide range of sectors – not just higher education – student experience is assessed mainly through feedback from surveys. Students are now exposed to numerous surveys throughout their study cycle for an award, and the question must be asked as to whether this has resulted in a corresponding improvement in student experience. The argument stands that new alternative methods might be more suited to identifying those issues that will better inform the future direction of small private higher education institutions and possibly larger institutions too.

Increasingly the burden of providing large amounts of statistical data as evidence of a standard of teaching and learning has 'swamped' academic and administrative staff. At least one of the case studies referred to in the following makes clear statements on the preparedness to seek out new approaches claiming, 'It is a common complaint among academic staff that the mountain of paperwork, the cumbersome procedures and the administrative burden have grown to proportions that are barely controllable' (Van de Walle, 2018). From one perspective it is not feasible that smaller institutions can substantiate an increasing number of personnel to address the various statistical reporting data requirements. The most obvious effect of this is the reallocation of precious resources away from the very learning and teaching activities such data is supposed to assist in improving. This has been extensively critiqued, particularly in the UK tertiary context, where the bureaucratic burden of quality upon universities was highlighted by authors such as Harvey, Jones, Watson, Brown and Mathias, particularly between the mid-1990s and mid-2000s (Brown, 2004; Mathias, 2004; Jones, 2003, Watson, 1995; Harvey, 1998, 2005). All these authors highlighted the burdensome, overlapping bureaucratic requirements of quality assurance which, they argued, may end up being detrimental to real quality.

There are voices emerging calling for reassessing established approaches to monitoring quality in the hope of improving educational outcomes for students. This leads us to a question: How then might small private higher education institutions that operate on the periphery of the larger universities identify critical issues for quality in learning and teaching? Narrative inquiry is a human-centred approach sensitive to complex issues and may provide an alternative approach to uncover nuances and identify critical issues in the experiences of learners across all fields of education. Narrative inquiry is better suited to small sample sizes whilst also being sensitive to the ways in which knowledge is developed. It identifies issues that have resulted in changed worldviews of participants and the interaction between thought and behaviour.

Other factors

Learning is a complex task and how learning occurs is a debated topic amongst educationalists (Hager, 2004; Brown and Palincsar, 1989; Winch, 1998; Schoenfeld, 1999). Winch (1998), for instance, argued that "the possibility of giving a scientific or even a systematic account of human learning is . . . mistaken" (p. 2) and that being a complex task in its own right challenges any research method that might be applied to learning and quality outcomes. A method that relies on a reductionist principle (reducing questions to a measurable statistic) may not provide the insight needed for future decisions.

Further with the growth of the numbers and types of higher education institutions (both government and privately funded), the diversity of factors that are associated with quality assurance increase proportionately. The types of institutions include a variety of not-for-profits, universities, specialised universities, for-profit providers and faith-based institutions which form part of an increasingly complex sector. New approaches to research in this context need to be able to cater for degrees of complexity.

In addition, changing political climates, economic downturns and increased regulatory activity combine to add to the level of complexity in a quality assurance agenda.

The need for new approaches to quality assurance in higher education

The appeal for new approaches to quality in higher education is increasing as the weaknesses in current methodologies are criticised by progressive institutions. Three examples are used to highlight this movement in exploring and adapting new approaches to quality in higher education. The first example is from Ghent University, a public research university located in Ghent, Belgium. The second example is derived from a keynote address by Professor David Lloyd, the current vice chancellor of the University of South Australia, addressing the future of higher education. The final example turns to the UK and an article written by Andrew Jack in February of 2019, discussing the toughest tests that universities will have to face, noting that '[f]ew countries beyond the US match the extent to which English higher education has been turned into a business over the past two decades'.

Each of these examples points to aspects of quality in different higher education contexts where narrative inquiry could be used.

Example 1: Ghent University, Belgium

Ghent University is a comprehensive research-intensive public university located in Belgium. It has close to 42,000 students, around 15,000 staff members and 11 faculties (divided into 86 departments).

In December 2018, the Ghent University's vice chancellor, Rik Van de Walle, argued in an online article (17 December 2018) that his university should be run by academics rather than by bureaucracy. Van de Walle described his intention and vision: of the university stepping out of the endless bureaucratic push that encouraged competition within the whole institution, between departments and individuals. He highlighted the cumbersome procedures and administrative burden placed on academics, the increasing emphasis on research outputs tied to fund allocation. Van de Walle expressed a belief that such an environment prevents collaboration between staff, implying that a prescriptive focus on bureaucratic procedures to demonstrate quality may in fact end up harming it.

Emphasising the return of 'academy' to academics rather than the bureaucracy, Van de Walle noted the impact of using the same metrics, templates and criteria across the entire higher education sector. He argued that a uniform approach to assessing all institutions attempts to make institutions the 'same' rather than encouraging difference, creativity and possible even innovation. He described his proposed new approach as follows:

> We [Ghent University] opt for a radically new model: those who perform well will be promoted, with a minimum of accountability and administrative effort and a maximum of freedom and responsibility. The quality of the individual human capital is given priority: talent must be nurtured and feel valued.

Van de Walle emphasised valuing the individual academics and their efforts. Performance indicators that are typically not well aligned with academic pursuits will be replaced with commitments based on collaboration supported by supervisors and paying more attention to 'well-being' at work.

Van de Walle further noted that the intense political pressures and debates around the funding of universities were harming institutions, and he argued that he would lead his institution away from that and was convinced that his new collegial approach would benefit the overall quality of his institution and people.

In summary, Van de Walle highlighted the constraints of current approaches associated with quality. He argued that the approaches commonly applied to universities by quality agencies funded by governments are to create a sector that is 'more of the same', where individual differences and strengths become increasingly indistinguishable. The emphasis Van de Walle placed on individual freedoms and commitments could be seen as a space for new approaches to quality and here could possibly be where a narrative inquiry approach might assist.

Example 2: University of South Australia

The University of South Australia has more than 31,000 students and 2,816 staff. It is a public research university and a member of the so-called Australian Technology Network of universities and has four academic divisions and six campuses.

Example 2 also broadly refers to quality in higher education and reflects on the future of higher education. It is derived from a keynote by the vice chancellor of the University of South Australia, Professor David Lloyd, at the Tertiary Education Quality and Standards Agency 2018 conference. Lloyd outlined his vision of the university of the future which, he argued, would continue in both teaching and research. He referred to Cardinal Newman, the founder of Trinity College Dublin, who described the role of university in his book *The Idea of a University*: 'to educate the intellect to reason well in all matters, to reach out for – and to grasp – the truth'.

Lloyd suggested that in the current era, the higher education sector still continues to be challenged by this statement. He argued that 'universities are [still] all working very hard to introduce such flexibility to our universities, to teach our students how to think, to reason, to seek out truth through their education – to overcome ignorance, to overcome timetables, and to excel'. He spoke to the need now, more than ever, that the future of higher must be contemplated.

In addressing the future of higher education, Lloyd gave several examples of directions taken by a variety of countries around the world:

- The French IdEx project, which is amalgamating institutions and 'enhancing human capital and backing it with additional money to improve the system, to take it beyond world class, not the application of cuts to stymie it and take it backwards';
- Investment made by the Republic of Ireland in education, done at a time of national financial troubles (invested 359 million Euros in research believing in the importance of education as underpinning a smart economy); and
- Canada, which has recently done something similar.

In summary, the examples offered by Lloyd highlighted the importance of investment in higher education rather than funding cuts. In addition, he highlighted the importance of human capital and of 'investment . . . around driving quality interdisciplinary collaboration across institutions . . . not rewarding competitive individualism'.

Lloyd provided the reasons why universities should continue in both research and teaching:

- Information is everywhere – knowledge is not. A university for the future must advance new knowledge through research.
- Funding research is an investment that leads to translation into industry.
- Cross-discipline and amalgamations generate research environment where breakthroughs happen.
- Transfer of knowledge occurs through the education of students as well as through partnerships, policy and public discourse.
- Progressing the concept of providing education 'on demand'.
- Learning will be chunked in increasingly smaller units of learning.
- The adoption of new ways to admit and assess students.

Lloyd contemplated the ways in which a university can continue to innovate in a 'highly regulated, monitored and evaluated system' (Lloyd, 2018). He suggested that governments, universities, industries and the public need to think about enabling strategies rather than making attempts to further prescribe the shape of universities in the future. He proposed that institutions should be more proactive in acting now rather than waiting for external drivers to force them to act.

Lloyd highlighted the importance of human capital and ways of working together, which are instrumental to the university of the future. In this, he remarked on Australian higher education but also his vision for his own institution. This alignment of human centredness and complexity of working as proposed by Lloyd and this broad topic, it may be argued, would suit investigation using a narrative inquiry method.

Example 3: Higher Education in the United Kingdom

In a *Financial Times* article (5 February 2019), Andrew Jack highlighted the wide range of issues faced by the UK higher education sector. Jack argued that, with the exception of the United States, few countries compared to the way higher education has been turned into a business over the last two decades. Jack highlighted the impact of the changed environment on higher education, making institutions which used to be very stable increasingly vulnerable.

The pressures echoed across the UK higher education sector include domestic political pressures, international competition, the value of higher education to a growing population, the growth of the student population, increase in the number of institutions and escalating costs.

Jack (2019) argued that Brexit, for instance, presents an ongoing concern and challenge for British higher education with regard to the decline in non-UK staff and uncertainties around EU research funding. Jack underlined a comment made by Russell Group universities' vice chancellors that Brexit would result in an academic, cultural and scientific setback to UK universities that would take decades for them to recover from.

Finally, Jack remarked on the debate concerning the relevance of higher education in the UK and the value it gives its students, including the wide variation in the quality and outcomes of degrees offered.

Example 3 would seem to offer a broad range of issues for a researcher investigating the quality of higher education. Narrative inquiry, it is argued, would offer a suitable method, enabling a sensitive approach to the diversity of factors impacting small and large, government and private institutions. At the very least, Jack's article prompts a need for research that would provide insight into the future of higher education.

Summary of examples

The examples discussed here highlight three issues that suggest that the application of a narrative inquiry research approach should be considered (if not justified) in researching topics associated with quality assurance in higher education.

In Example 1, Van de Walle highlighted the value of human capital, emphasising the importance of human centredness in the future success of higher education. It is this trust in human capital more than processes and templates imposed by bureaucrats that Van de Walle believed will improve the quality and outcomes of higher education for students.

In Example 2, Lloyd debated the need to be different and not have all higher education institutions cast in to the same mould. Lloyd pointed out that emphasis should be placed on enabling strategies rather than further efforts to prescribe the shape of higher education. In doing so, Lloyd identified the need to work with various parts of the community and the associated complexity. Addressing complexity in human-related activity is a feature that can be explored well by the narrative inquiry method.

In Example 3, Jack argued that the UK higher education sector is facing a crisis and requires new approaches. In doing so, he underlined the existence of a broad range of topics that would benefit from being investigated using methodologies that are sensitive to a diversity of factors, including human factors. Narrative inquiry is referred to in the literature as being a methodology that is sensitive to factors that are not readily identified by more traditional quantitative methodologies.

All the three examples highlighted the need for new research approaches to address the future needs of higher education, providing insight to what might constitute criteria for quality assurance in the future.

What might a narrative research interview instrument look like?

Quality assurance in higher education has as its focus evidence that draws on systems and processes that institutions rely on to deliver courses. Reviews of quality assurance in higher education, such as Wilger's (1997), and the websites of quality assurance agencies, such as the UK's Quality Assurance Agency and the Australian Tertiary Education Quality and Standards Agency, further inform the researcher of the type of evidence associated with quality in higher education. The association of evidence with quantitative data is prominent. Whether this approach will be adequate in addressing the needs of higher education in the future is debatable, but a refocus on the stories of students at the very least would provide another way of viewing quality in higher education and the changes it might suggest. This focus on students in researching quality in higher education is further highlighted by a number of authors.

Ryan (2015) stated that given that students are at the centre of higher education – and they invest time and money in the system – involving them could improve quality assurance processes. Bennet (2001) highlighted the role of the student in assessing quality in higher education. Morgan (2019) argued how the higher education market has become increasingly competitive and students have become more demanding and better informed about what services and support they expect to receive whilst studying at university. On the other hand, whilst the role and significance of student voice in quality assurance processes in the current times is undeniable and many academics acknowledge this (Bishop *et al.*, 2012), there is also an argument for counterbalancing this voice with the academic voice, as frequently academics at the coalface of teaching and learning, particularly in Anglophone countries, such as the UK and Australia, are not heard and supported. This was raised by British academics in research on quality in higher education conducted by Mertova (2008). Research by Green and Mertova (2014, 2011, 2010) has also underlined the fact that less senior academics in Australian universities were frequently neglected when delivering frontline teaching. This was recently (9 May 2019) acknowledged in a policy note by Rachel Hewitt for the Oxford think-tank, Higher Education Policy Institute (HEPI), underlining the need for supporting the well-being of not only students but also academics.

The student voice and academic voice are two complex aspects of quality in higher education suitable for investigation by the narrative inquiry method. Such an investigation should not be restricted just to students and academics, as the higher education community includes a lot more complex web of voices representing many other stakeholder groups.

Possible individual participant questions

What might be some questions that researchers may consider when interviewing a student to capture stories of their experience and relate those to issues associated with quality assurance? In asking questions, the researchers will draw on the underpinnings of narrative inquiry, seeking to tap into those events that initiated some change in a student's understanding or impacted their worldview.

Questions which encourage participants to reflect on their experiences and recount stories will be the source of inquiry for the researcher. Table 7.1 lists some questions that might form the basis for further elaborations and refinements by the researcher interested in quality assurance.

The questions in this table serve as a starting point for an interviewer and should be modified according to the context and experience of the student. For example, questions asked some time following the completion of a course will serve as an account of reflection on the course as a whole, whereas interviewing a student whilst completing the course may focus more on a component or subject level.

Perhaps simply the use of the definition of a critical event may serve as the best means for acquiring stories of experience of students related to quality in higher education.

TABLE 7.1 Quality assurance and researcher questions

What was the main barrier you faced in successfully completing your studies?
When did you feel you were most noticed?
What was the learning experience like for you? What do you recall as a significant time in your learning experience?
Was there one instance that powerfully impacted you and your experience of learning?
Was there anything you wished had been different? What initiated that desire for change?
What has made the most difference to you as a learner in higher education?
What story do you recount when telling others about your learning experience?
What were the best features of your programme of study?
What feature had the most impact on you? Why?

May *et al.* (2008) discussed the impact of a critical event on a student's actions and experiences and were of the view that this would be an event with a subsequent impact on attitudes, skills and knowledge. They believed that experience of a critical event may arise from involvement in a project and interaction with a faculty staff or fellow students. May *et al.* (2008) provide a sample of their interview questions, which may also relate to investigating quality in higher education. Following is a sample of these questions.

1   *Have you had a 'critical moment' (at . . . or in a prior educational setting)?* _____
    Yes _____ *No* _____
2   *If you have had a critical moment, please specify when it occurred (while at . . . , in high school, in a specific course) and whether it was positive or negative:*

    _____

    _____

3   *If you have had a critical moment, what caused the 'critical moment'?* _____

    _____

    _____

    _____

4   *If you have had a critical moment, how did you deal with the 'critical moment' and what were the outcomes? (e.g., Did it sway you away from or into a certain major?)*

    _____

    _____

    _____

May et al. (2008)

Possible domains for developing further interview questions

There are a variety of domains of student experience that may be suitable for researchers in quality assurance to consider.

Table 7.2 lists a sample of domains relevant to the student experience based on the aspects covered in student satisfaction surveys.

TABLE 7.2 Domains relevant to student experience

Support services
Teaching quality
Courses
Assessment
Feedback
Preparation for employment
Relevance
Workload
Resources

A review of the various country-based quality agencies by researchers will identify further domains that may assist the development of questionnaires probing the student experience in higher education. For example, in Australia, the Social Research Centre's Quality Indicators for Learning and Teaching (QILT) website outlines the domains related to student experience. The domains currently used by QILT include the overall quality of educational experience, teaching quality, learner engagement, learning resources, student support and skills development. These domains may not only assist the formulation of questions to elicit critical events but provide a useful framework for classifying and analysing the stories of experience that are collected by researchers. Possibly the biggest benefit of using the domains is their assistance in considering the various facets of the student experience and the types of critical events that may contribute to researching the quality of higher education at a local, country and even global level.

While researching quality in higher education, a good starting point for the researcher may be to develop a matrix of the relationship(s) between the concept of quality and the investigated domains. The researcher can then develop questions against an explanatory and defensible framework providing an explanation of the assumptions underlying the development of questions to assist the identification of critical events as well as like and other events explained elsewhere in this book.

Summary

Why use a narrative method to research quality assurance in higher education? This chapter argued that there is a critical need to re-examine the direction of higher education and the student experience. Three examples were provided to illustrate this need whilst also identifying levels of dissatisfaction with current approaches and metrics associated with quality and voicing the need to urgently identify and adopt new approaches to learning and teaching in higher education.

The chapter further outlined the possible angles and directions which a researcher into quality in higher education may take. Researchers would first be encouraged to get an understanding of the range of domains and aspects of quality and clearly articulate those most relevant to their topic of investigation. Finally, an approach to developing a conceptual framework for questions addressed in the research was outlined. This framework incorporates a matrix with the conceptual components of quality on an axis with the various domains associated with quality. This approach will aid the researcher in preparing research questions and subsequent coding or classification. In conclusion, the chapter's main argument was that a narrative inquiry approach to researching quality in higher education has considerable value and potential for higher education.

This chapter argued for the utility of narrative inquiry as a research and evaluation method in the complex area of quality in higher education and suggested ways that researchers might go about planning, starting and conducting research on quality in higher education, as well as proposing narrative inquiry as an alternative method of evaluating quality in higher education. The following chapter discusses and illustrates how a critical event narrative method was used in research investigating academic perspectives of internationalisation and quality in three different cultural contexts: Czech, English and Australian.

8

A CRITICAL EVENT NARRATIVE INQUIRY

Internationalisation and quality in a comparative higher education context

Introduction

Internationalisation and quality have been on the agendas of higher education institutions around the world as the key policy drivers for some time. Quality in higher education has gained attention particularly over the last three decades (Westerheijden *et al.*, 1994). Internationalisation of higher education has developed virtually in parallel with quality (Van der Wende and Westerheijden, 2001). This timeline is relevant particularly for the Anglophone and Western European higher education systems. These trends emerged in the Central and Eastern European region about two decades ago in the case of quality and approximately a decade ago in the case of internationalisation.

However, internationalisation and quality have developed their separate systemic characteristics (Van der Wende and Westerheijden, 2001), and it was only in the 1990s that links on the policy and practice levels started being developed (Campbell and van der Wende, 2000). Despite there being a significant body of research on higher education quality, a lack of focus on the academic voice in quality was highlighted by Newton (2001), Lomas (2007), Cartwright (2007) and Mertova (2008). Similarly, a lack of research on the academic perceptions of internationalisation has also been emphasised (Dewey and Duff, 2009).

This chapter discusses how critical event narrative inquiry method was used to investigate the complex phenomena of internationalisation and quality in higher education, with a focus on senior academics' perspectives on internationalisation and quality in three higher education contexts: Czech, Australian and English. The research focused on these particular perspectives based on previous literature, indicating that senior academics (such as heads of schools and associate deans academic) played significant roles in instigating and implementing change in higher education and yet they were often 'neglected' (Bell, 2004; Anderson and Johnson, 2006; Green and Mertova, 2010).

The research was instigated partly by a previous study investigating quality in higher education, where Czech academics drew a direct link between quality enhancement and internationalisation (Mertova, 2008) and partly also by literature indicating a lack of research on academic perceptions of internationalisation (Dewey and Duff, 2009). Although the study investigated internationalisation and quality, internationalisation turned out to be the dominant focus, and thus this chapter mainly focuses on academic perceptions of internationalisation. The following sections outline the understandings of internationalisation and quality broadly relevant to the research.

Internationalisation in higher education

Internationalisation in higher education is a phenomenon which has become a widespread and strategically significant aspect of higher education (Van der Wende and Westerheijden, 2001) over the past nearly three decades. Internationalisation was pioneered particularly in the Anglophone higher education systems, such as Australia and the UK.

Throughout the 1990s, significant shifts in foreign policies, particularly in the Anglophone countries, have occurred where education started being treated as an export commodity. Prior to that, education 'exported' overseas was primarily seen as a development activity or cultural programme (such as the Colombo Plan in Australia). This change led to a search for effective ways of improving the quality of provision and thus maintaining a 'competitive edge' (Knight, 1999). This was also a point where the links between internationalisation and quality started being more consciously developed. Internationalisation in Czech higher education started being forged more systematically, particularly on the mobility front, in the early 2000s (Ministry of Education, Youth and Sports, 2001a; Ministry of Education, Youth and Sports, 2001b).

Internationalisation has always existed in higher education, despite this renewed attention to the phenomenon, only perhaps more utilitarian and politicised meanings and values have been ascribed to it in the more recent times. In some form, universities have always been influenced by social, cultural and physical (the 'wandering' scholar) movements, which have given them the ability not to confine themselves within particular spatial boundaries (van Damme, 2001). However, there have been some notable exceptions which relate to this research – for instance, the universities in undemocratic political systems, such as the former Communist regimes of Central and Eastern Europe, where these spatial boundaries were firmly closed for over 40 years (between the late 1940s and 1980s).

For the purposes of the broad focus of the research, Van Damme's (2001) outline of the forms of internationalisation was utilised. According to him, internationalisation incorporates the following forms:

- student mobility – includes outgoing as well as incoming students;
- teaching staff mobility;

- internationalisation of curricula;
- branch campuses – Van Damme indicated that this phenomenon is more widespread among Anglophone countries; and
- institutional cooperation agreements and networks – this includes collaboration between universities as not a particularly new phenomenon, as well as institutional cooperation in the field of teaching as a relatively recent one.

Knight (2004) described four different dimensions of internationalisation, which were perceived as complementary. They are the following:

- *Activity* dimension – internationalisation as specific activities or programmes; this perception was associated with internationalisation in the 1970s and 1980s;
- *Competency* dimension – internationalisation in terms of the knowledge, skills, attitudes and values of the students;
- *Ethos* dimension – relates to the culture and climate of the organisation to support particular principles and goals; and
- *Process* dimension – relates to an integration of international, intercultural and global aspects into academic programmes as well as guiding policies and procedures within the institution.

Australian and English academics who participated in the study discussed here referred to all the forms and dimensions of internationalisation. Czech academics referred largely to student and staff mobility and the *activity* dimension of Knight's definition. The explanation for this may be perhaps less extensive experience with internationalisation within the Czech tertiary context but also the particular cultural, historical, political and socio-economic context. The following section describes the methodology utilised in the study.

Quality in higher education

Quality in higher education has gained increased attention virtually in parallel with internationalisation (Van der Wende and Westerheijden, 2001). The focus on quality in higher education has resulted from a range of competing factors, including the following:

- political control over higher education (exerted particularly by national governments);
- growth in the number of students in higher education (including general changes in the student population and their expectations); and
- financial control on the part of national governments, frequently related to the previous two factors (Stoddart, 2004; Harvey, 1998; Brown, 2004; Green, 1994).

Quality monitoring has become a mechanism for governments worldwide to tackle these competing factors and frequently also to disguise the dominant focus on accountability rather than enhancement (Harvey, 2005). Among higher education institutions around the world, there have been various responses to this trend, ranging from implementing direct quality measurement scales to conducting self-audit processes. Increasingly, the rationale for quality development has been driven by funding mechanisms, accreditation, keeping pace with international practice, national audits and other trends, such as massive growth in higher education and influences of information technology (Barnett, 1992; Harvey and Green, 1993; Morley, 1997; Lomas, 2000; Harvey, 2004, 2005). The rationale for internationalisation has coincided with that of quality in virtually all aspects.

There is a broad range of definitions of quality. For the purposes of this chapter, a summarised understanding is given. Quality is a complex and multifaceted concept. According to Lomas (2004), there are two main understandings of quality: quality assurance and quality enhancement. Quality assurance is oriented mainly towards the product or service being of good standard. It is a 'preventative' measure, which is 'regarded as a means of improving overall quality', and it relates to the notion of 'fitness for purpose'. Quality enhancement, on the other hand, is 'directly concerned with adding value, improving quality . . . and implementing transformational change'.

Harvey and Green (1993) defined six notions of quality:

- *Traditional* concept – associated with exceptionally high standards;
- Concept associated with *consistency* and '*zero defects*' – associated with process and a set of specifications;
- *Fitness for purpose* – relates to a product or service meeting its purpose;
- *Value for money* – concerns accountability;
- *Transformative* process; and
- *Pragmatic* approach – as a range of qualities (i.e. institution of high standard in relation to one factor may be low in relation to another).

The understanding of quality academics in this research mainly referred to was quality enhancement and a combination of the *traditional* and *transformative* concepts of quality. They understood this very positively, although some English and Australians also understood quality as quality assurance, which they perceived mainly as negative and limiting.

Methodology

The research was conducted through semi-structured, face-to-face interviews with senior academics in English, Australian and Czech higher education. It involved 81 interviews, and the participants represented disciplines of education, higher education, law, history, English, English literature, classics, philosophy, Australian studies, political science, sociology, psychology, media studies, geography, business and economics, medicine, engineering, maths, physics and chemistry. The broadest range of disciplines was covered at the most senior management level; at the faculty and school levels, the disciplines represented mostly included humanities, arts and social science disciplines. The interviews lasted between 30 and 45 minutes. The research was conducted between June 2010 and June 2011. The interviews were recorded, subsequently transcribed and analysed. The interviewees were given pseudonyms to protect their identities.

Interview data was analysed utilising a *critical event* narrative inquiry method. The essence of the method is in identification of *critical events* in professional practice of individuals; in this case, it was the academics. The identification of *critical events* was negotiated between the researcher, interviewees and at least two independent researchers.

As was explained earlier in this book, a *critical event* is an event which would have significantly impacted on professional practice of, for instance, an academic. Such an event might have entirely or considerably changed the academic's perception of their professional practice or even their worldview. *Critical event* can only be identified retrospectively, and such an event would have happened in an unplanned and unstructured manner. The causes of a critical event might be 'internal' or 'external' to professional practice of an individual, or entirely personal. A critical event has a unique, illustrative and confirmatory nature in relation to an investigated phenomenon. Critical events in professional practice of academics in the present research were elicited through semi-structured, face-to-face interviews with the individuals.

According to the degree of significance and unique characteristics, *critical events* in professional practice of academics were further distinguished as *critical*, *like* and *other* events. Narratives that were collected through narrative inquiry interviews were then analysed and events in them were identified as *critical*, *like* and *other*.

An event which has a similar level of significance as a *critical* event, however, is not as unique as the critical event, and an event which further illustrated, confirmed and/or repeated the experience of the critical event is referred to as a *like* event. A review of the *like* events is useful in confirming and/or broadening issues arising from the critical event (Webster, 1998). *Critical* and *like* events are distinguished according to the criteria outlined in Tables 8.1 and 8.2.

TABLE 8.1 Features of a 'critical' event in professional practice

Feature	Presence/absence
a) Has a major impact on people involved	√
b) Is unplanned and unanticipated	√
c) Is only identified after the event	√
d) May have life-changing consequences	√ x
e) May reveal patterns of well-defined stages	√ x
f) May be intensely personal with strong emotional involvement	√ x

Note: √ indicates presence; x indicates absence.

TABLE 8.2 Features of a 'like' event in professional practice

Feature	Presence/absence
a) Has a major impact on people involved	x
b) Is unplanned and unanticipated	√ x
c) Is only identified after the event	√
d) May have life-changing consequences	x
e) May reveal patterns of well-defined stages	x
f) May be intensely personal with strong emotional involvement	x
Additional features	**Presence**
aa) Not as unique (as critical event)	√
ab) Repeats and/or illustrates experience (of critical event)	√

Note: √ indicates presence; x indicates absence.

TABLE 8.3 Features of 'other' event in professional practice

Feature	Presence/absence
a) Has a major impact on people involved	x
b) Is unplanned and unanticipated	√ x
c) Is only identified after the event	√ x
d) May have life-changing consequences	x
e) May reveal patterns of well-defined stages	x
f) May be intensely personal with strong emotional involvement	x
Additional features	**Presence**
aaa) Further background information	√

Note: √ indicates presence; x indicates absence.

Further, confirmatory event(s) that may or may not have taken place at the same time as the *critical* and/or *like* events are referred to as *other* event(s). Typically, such events relate to other background information which may have revealed the same or related issues. The criteria which distinguish *other* events are described in Table 8.3. These *other* events are interwoven in the analysis of the *critical* and *like* events (Webster, 1998). *Critical*, *like* and *other* events may occur within the narrative of a single interview but more often would occur across a number of different interviews.

Distinguishing *critical*, *like* and *other* events provides a way of approaching the complexity and extent of data that might be collected using a qualitative research method. A common question in qualitative research is how to manage the amount of collected data. The identification and distinguishing of individual events provides one way to assist the researcher in this (Webster and Mertova, 2007).

Limitations of the study

There were a number of limitations to the study. These limitations largely do not bear on the actual research method. First, the limited time (and resources) impacted on the number and range of institutions covered in the research. Related to the previous PhD research study, there was not enough scope in this study to consider distinctions in approaches to internationalisation and quality of different types of institutions in the three higher education systems (e.g. 'old' vs. 'new', i.e. post-92 institutions, former polytechnics) in the English system; 'research-intensive', Go8 universities vs. the 'technology network' vs. 'regional' etc. in Australia and 'metro-politan' vs. 'regional' institutions in the Czech system Further, there was not enough scope to have a representative sample of the widest range of disciplines, and the widest range of disciplines occurred only among the most senior institutional lead-ers. Another limitation might have been the predominant focus on senior academ-ics and leaders, which was explained earlier. Finally, Czech academics and leaders were generally less responsive to invitations to participate in research.

Identifying *critical events* in academic narratives

As explained earlier, *critical events* can be distinguished as *critical*, *like* and *other* according to their level of criticality. This section provides examples of different levels of critical-ity of events across the three higher education systems to help illustrate the types of events. It should be noted that not all academic narratives contained all types of *critical events*. Academics are referred to by pseudonyms to protect their identities.

Critical *events*

Krystian (senior Czech university executive; disciplines – history and political science; tertiary experience – over 20 years) remembered a *critical* event which he experienced during the Communist era in the 1980s when he had attended an underground university, which was run through a series of lectures and seminars organised in private flats in his hometown. These were secretly organised for six years prior to 1989. They were given by outstanding British philosophers, political philosophers and sociologists. He felt that this experience has given him much more substantive knowledge than a study at a communist university: 'for the first time, I've experienced a very differ-ent form of debate and freedom of opinion and this has in some ways significantly shaped my future academic and research direction'.

Krystian referred to another *critical* event which, although it repeated some of the features of the previous event, incorporated all the features of criticality in a very different context and focused more on cultural than professional aspects. In 1990, he spent some time at a German university. Although the professional aspects were quite important, the cultural context and differences were a lot more signifi-cant for him, as he said that it was the notions of 'strangeness and loneliness in a cul-tural context where he understood the language perfectly but did not understand the humour and other subtleties'. Such experiences, he believed, were not possible to pass on without the actual experience.

Krystian's first *critical* event did involve enhancement of pedagogical practices, although there was a strong underlying political and cultural context. In his second *critical* event, Krystian highlighted the cultural aspects of his experience.

James (an English professor; discipline – education; tertiary experience – over 30 years) referred to a *critical* event, his first sabbatical abroad, and he referred to this as *internationalising himself* when he spent a month in Malaysia and nine months in Australia. He referred to this experience as a 'major turning point' in his career and explained that 'it wasn't the specific stuff – I wrote an important paper but it was just brought in my mind that there was a much bigger world out there'; he went on to say that he has developed 'lots of ongoing work in Malaysia. The Australian one – that's absolutely ongoing, I have lots of good contacts there, so lots of collaborations with Australia'.

James also experienced a second *critical* event which related to a capacity-building project in an institute of education on the Indian subcontinent, which was undertaken by his current department. This experience has introduced him to a different and much more professional set of practices than he was used to from his previous institutions.

Although James's *critical* events related to the professional, they predominantly highlighted the cultural aspects of these events. James very likely would not have been able to reflect on his professional practices in such a way had he not had these experiences. In his story, James has also referred to an *other* event related to the lack of foreign language proficiency among the majority of his English colleagues (certainly within his discipline of education); the event is outlined later on (please refer to *Other* events, p. 107).

Mark (a senior Australian academic; disciplines – anthropology and sociology; tertiary experience – over 20 years) for many years travelled extensively through Asia, the Pacific and India, and, during that time, he experienced a *critical event* or even a series, as he spoke of experiences which had been highly significant in his life. In his words:

> I had to face who I was . . . and they [the experiences] spoke to me about difference, similarities, the importance of language, to be able to handle ones fears, uncertainties in sometimes quite difficult situations; they also made me appreciate learning, the need to learn from others; I probably also had the advantage of studying anthropology, when I started initially, and anthropology gave me that terrific breadth of understanding culture and then I saw some of those changes away from traditional anthropology towards much more critical anthropology.

Mark's series of *critical* events have also involved cultural aspects and engaged him as a human being. These then subsequently impacted on his professional practices later on, which took him to remote aboriginal communities in Australia and enabled him to relate to and help in solving the issues these communities faced.

Like *events*

Anna (a senior Australian academic; disciplines – history and English literature; tertiary experience – over 20 years) described a *like* event which was situated in her current institution. The event involved her teaching a course on postgraduate supervision and delivering a module on Indigenous issues. Anna understood internationalisation in its broadest sense to include indigenisation within the Australian context. She invited an Indigenous colleague to talk about Indigenous knowledge and bringing that into the university as a discipline; one participant stood up and said: 'I'm not sure that this belongs to the university, I mean plumbing isn't taught in the university, is it?' Anna was astounded at the arrogance and the lack of understanding about history and culture, and she felt that such an attitude to Indigenous knowledge would be similarly reflected in the academics' attitudes to, for example, Eastern knowledge, African knowledge or South American knowledges. This event has repeated Anna's previous critical event experience also related to Indigenous education.

Claudia (a senior English academic; discipline – education; tertiary experience – over 30 years) experienced a *like* event when she worked at an Australian university; the dean of her faculty came to her and told her: 'you are going to fly to Malaysia, deliver a course within a week and then you'll fly back', and she agreed but requested, 'I fly out a week before so that I can look at their teaching and adapt my teaching accordingly and then I want to stay the week after so that I can evaluate how they've perceived my teaching'. The dean disagreed, so Claudia refused to travel to Malaysia. She was outraged at the arrogance but also a certain naivety in totally disregarding the cultural context. This event has repeated some of Claudia's experiences from the start of her career.

Marek (senior Czech university leader; discipline – sociology; tertiary experience – over 20 years) discussed one of his sabbaticals spent overseas as a significant moment in his academic career. This event repeated some of the features of his previous time spent overseas, and this event was mainly professionally focused.

Both Anna's and Claudia's *like* events underlined the significance of the cultural contexts impacting on their pedagogical practices. Marek's event highlighted mainly his own professional development.

Other *events*

Alexandra's other event (Australian university senior leader; discipline – human geography; tertiary experience – over 20 years) related to learning languages in an Anglophone context. She highlighted the significance of learning foreign languages for her university staff, even at the administrative level, and her university offered courses in other languages for staff. Alexandra believed that languages other than English had a vital role to play in internationalising endeavours.

The *other* event described by *James* related to learning foreign languages among English academics. He acknowledged that being in Europe, it was vital to learn other languages, although he regretted that he has not done so himself. He related his situation to many other British academics for whom it was fairly

> typical that they don't speak any other European languages or not to the
> level one could work in; related to the educational system which is English

oriented, so takes you around the English-speaking world, and leaves you actually blind to Europe.

Richard (a senior Czech academic and administrator; discipline – English language and literature; tertiary experience – over 30 years) discussed an *other* event related to internationalisation in a large research-intensive university in the Czech Republic. He perceived internationalisation as linked to a number of aspects of quality. One aspect that was being debated in his institution concerned the approaches to gaining more international students through delivering educational programmes either in Czech or in English. Such a language aspect, for instance, would not represent a significant quality measure in the Anglophone systems, as a great majority of – if not all – programmes offered to foreign students would be delivered in English. Richard further outlined how the language of delivery would be strongly related to offering programmes to particular groups of international students:

1   Programmes delivered in Czech would be targeted at Central and Eastern European students who would be able to master Czech with the help of a short language course (as they would be mainly speakers of other Slavonic languages).
2   Programmes delivered in English would be targeted more at other overseas students mainly from the 'Western world'.

Richard pointed out that insisting on delivering programmes only in Czech was related to a kind of 'self-satisfaction' attitude among some Czech academics, who felt that the quality of their programmes did not need further improvement. The delivery of programmes in English was, however, associated with certain 'fears' of some academics that weaknesses in the content and style of delivery of their programmes (normally taught in Czech) would be revealed by offering these in English, as these programmes would be more easily comparable to other similar programmes delivered in English in other higher education systems around the world. Therefore, the academic believed that the aspect of the language of delivery was felt as a powerful quality measure in his institution.

A great majority of the different types of events described by the previously mentioned academics have involved them in a reflection on their professional practices as impacted by cultural and contextual differences. Their experiences and reflections were intertwined throughout their professional practices. The Czech academic, Marek, was the only one who did not engage in a deeper reflection. His experience was relatively typical of the majority of senior Czech academics interviewed for this project. His lack of reflection might have been caused by the relatively limited range of experiences in internationalisation and perhaps also internationalisation of his subject area. The explanation for this may be perhaps less extensive experience with internationalisation within Czech tertiary institutions caused by the cultural, socio-economic, political and historical context. Krystian's and Richard's life trajectories were perhaps slightly unusual for the Czech context, which enabled them to be more reflective, with Krystian being involved in an underground university and Richard having been born and educated in Canada.

Summary of overall research findings and conclusions

Eliciting *critical events*, the study uncovered a number of *general/common* aspects in internationalising higher education and *culture-specific* aspects particular to the individual higher education systems. These were perceived as having some or, in some cases, significant relevance for quality. These aspects related to the examples of events given in this chapter but also more broadly to events described by other senior academics who have been interviewed as part of the study.

General/common aspects included, for instance, the following:

• Concern about the hegemony of the English language; the lack of knowledge of other languages flattening the experiences of cultural, historical and social contexts (e.g. in relation to researching particular topics or when taking part in exchanges or studies abroad). This was also previously highlighted for example by Marginson (2007) and Green and Mertova (2009);
• Adopting Western pedagogies and approaches without considering the local contexts does not necessarily improve practices (may for example result in the so-called 'reverse cultural shock' – related to students studying within Anglophone cultural contexts and returning to their native countries).

Culture-specific aspects included, for example, the following:

• Internationalisation as an aspect of quality enhancement in Czech higher education related to the introduction of programmes in the English language;
• A form of internationalisation as a quality enhancement strategy in the Czech context through attracting elite students from neighbouring Slavonic countries (e.g. Slovakia, Russia) to study in Czech alongside Czech students;
• Within the Australian context, indigenisation of teaching and learning as a broader understanding of internationalisation (related to developing intercultural competencies in staff and students); difficulties and resistance related to the lack of 'moral skill and will' (Schwartz, 2013).

Academics across the three higher education systems (as also outlined in the previous examples of events described by academics) highlighted the notions of *being challenged, put into a very different context, being taken out of their comfort zone, being able to accept and accommodate difference and being able to listen and learn*, which were perhaps the key ingredients enabling the academics to reflect on and utilise their experiences in their pedagogical practices. The academics also believed that the cultural context matters – either in adopting (Czech HE) or in proposing (English and Australian HE) particular pedagogical or other institutional models. Czech academics perceived internationalisation as a quality enhancement strategy either through the need to improve their own teaching material when required to teach their courses in English (with some parallels in other non-English-speaking countries), and be thus more open to external criticism, or through bringing in elite students from neighbouring Slavonic countries.

The Czech academics arguably had the least experience with a broader range of forms of internationalisation among the three groups, which might explain the uncritical and unreflective attitudes towards internationalisation among some of them. This may to a degree also be explained by the particular cultural, historical, political and socio-economic context of the Czech Republic as a conservative, relatively mono-cultural country with a very low mobility of the population, including the academic population. In comparison, English and Australian academics were more sceptical and critical of internationalisation and its links to quality, which could be ascribed to their particular cultural, historical and political circumstances, which some academics discussed in detail. Czech academics mainly perceived internationalisation as student and staff mobility (there may be some parallels with other, for example, European higher education systems but also Australian HE – for more details, see Green and Mertova, 2016). Very few Czech academics discussed transformations in teaching and learning; and if they did, these were mainly related to transformation of teaching methods and techniques, which would also require change in attitudes to some degree. Australian and English academics focused more on attitudes and values.

This chapter has discussed how a critical event narrative inquiry was applied in the study of academic perspectives of two, in some instances, related phenomena, namely internationalisation and quality in three higher education contexts. As was indicated through the range of *critical events*, a great majority of academics within the three examined systems have pointed to the complexities of developing international and intercultural competencies related to their personal lives and academic trajectories as well as to the particular historical, cultural, political and socio-economic contexts of the higher education systems within which they operated, highlighting some important aspects of internationalisation in higher education with relevance to quality. It is hoped that this chapter has given researchers some guidance on how to go about investigating complex topics within higher education, such as internationalisation and quality.

9

A FRAMEWORK FOR NARRATIVE RESEARCH

Review of a critical event approach to narrative

This book, so far, has provided researchers with a working understanding of the use of storytelling in research. The previous chapter showed how the critical event narrative inquiry method was applied to investigating the academic perspectives of internationalization and quality in three different cultural contexts. As we have previously indicated, the literature on storytelling and, more generally, narrative inquiry is dispersed. In this chapter we outline the features and aspects of a critical event narrative inquiry method that we argue is applicable to investigating a wide range complex and human-centred issues within a wide range of disciplinary contexts. One main reason for writing the second edition of this book a decade on is to present an approach that is useful to researchers interested in using a storytelling or narrative approach in their research.

The main feature of the approach described in this book is the prominence and usefulness of a storytelling approach to human-centred research. We assert that storytelling is a natural and common form of human communication and that storytelling is used to communicate those elements of experience that have had a profound impact on an individual. Further, these elements or events provide a means for investigating issues relevant to human activity that other, more traditional, methodologies are unlikely to uncover. As a way of researching the events contained in storytelling, we propose a critical event approach to assist the researcher in finding ways of uncovering these issues.

At the core of a critical event approach are the ways in which critical events can be exposed. We have asserted in previous chapters that, through the use of well-timed questions, participants in a research project retell their understanding of events that have occurred in their professional (and possibly private) lives and, perhaps, have changed their perspective on their current and future professional practice.

Perhaps the most difficult aspect of storytelling as a research method for the researcher is understanding and gaining an overview of the framework in which narrative research is conducted. This is hardly surprising given the complexity with which it deals and the difficulty of superimposing a framework on something that is so 'human' and thus variable. Nonetheless, we do now provide one such overview for the researcher to adopt, adapt or further develop.

A framework for the researcher

Because narrative inquiry is a method that has many constituent parts, it is useful to provide a visual representation of the methodology outlined in this book (Figure 9.1). At the highest levels of the framework are two factors that both govern and justify the methodology: the themes of *human centredness* and the *complexity* of human experience. The methodology contains four constituent parts: research *processes*, *negotiations* that occur, *risks* that may arise and preparation and auditing of *results*. The next section considers each of these constituent parts in turn.

Processes

Possibly the largest and the most complex of the constituent parts of this method, the research *processes* include three sub-constituents, each then broken down to a further level or levels (Figure 9.2). Processes contain *tools*, *criteria* and *structure*.

Tools

Tools comprise the number of possible data-gathering instruments available and thereby outline the instruments the researcher elects to use. Any reporting of the methodology will address the selection of instruments and their relevance to the research questions. These tools include observation, survey (limited), documentation (including letters, curricula and policies), interviews and transcripts. Not all of these will necessarily be used within the scope of any one research project.

Criteria

The *criteria* of narrative research include *verisimilitude, apparency* and *transferability* of the research. Much of this has to do with establishing the *authenticity* and *truthfulness* of the research. One of the distinguishing implications for the researcher is that there is a need for a well-referenced trail available for any reader to access the results and stories collected by the researcher. This essentially requires an indexing system that will allow any interested reader to locate a place or section of text within any transcripts or records provided by the researcher.

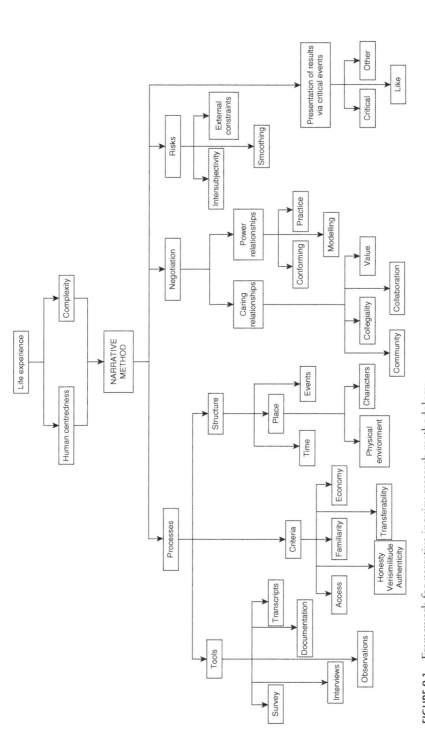

FIGURE 9.1 Framework for narrative inquiry research methodology

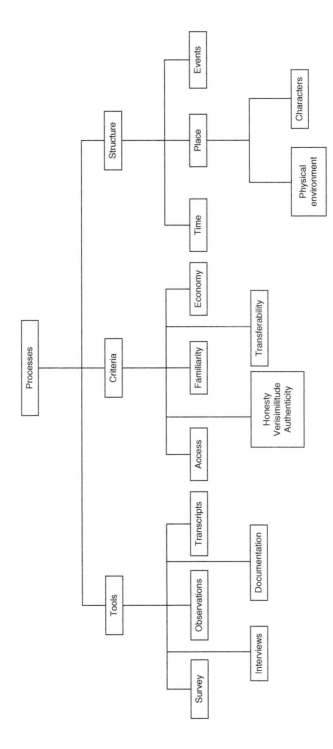

FIGURE 9.2 Outline of narrative inquiry processes

Structure

The research portrays the context and the setting by referring to those elements that combine to form an image of the *structure* in which the research took place. We have found that the three categories of *time*, *place* and *events* provide a rich and informative background for readers of the research.

* Every step of the research occurs at a particular moment of *time*. Time is essential to explaining plot or the unfolding of events.
* *Place* is a description of the research environment. It may include a description of the physical layout and the locations of various activities that are undertaken by participants in the study. Its purpose is essentially to familiarise the reader with the context of the research. 'Behind the scenes' information can accompany the description of place – details of background facilities, support staff and other key personnel.
* Each research *event* occurs at a specific time and place. The unfolding of these events creates the plot of the research.

Drawing substantially on approaches used in literary criticism, the *structure* attempts to set the scene in which the research occurs. It enables a picture to be drawn not only of the main characters but also of the setting in which they work and the structures and systems that impinge on and influence them. Perhaps most importantly, this approach stresses the human component of the research, as it explains the context and events in which characters within the research are placed.

Processes: a summary

All of the processes described combine to form a description of the context and the instruments used in conducting the research. Perhaps the most distinguishing emphasis between this and other descriptions of the narrative method is its human-centred approach, emphasising the interest in participants, their relationships, the structures they work within and the instruments used in an attempt to capture their stories of experience.

Negotiation

Negotiation, by definition, involves relationships (Figure 9.3). Two helpful categories in describing such relationships within the research context are the following:

* caring relationships; and
* empowering relationships.

Caring relationships in the research context refer to those that involve elements of collegiality, community and collaboration or are valued by those participating

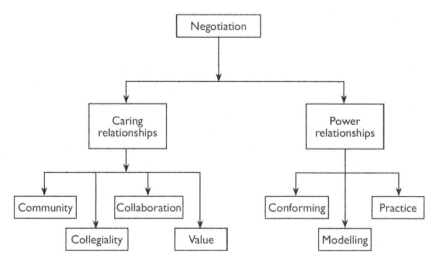

FIGURE 9.3 Outline of narrative inquiry negotiation

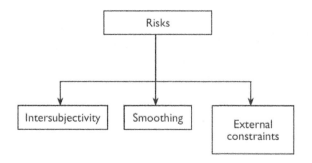

FIGURE 9.4 Outline of narrative inquiry risks

in the research. *Empowering relationships* are those that involve a chain of authority and the need to conform to it, the need to represent the home institution of the researcher responsibly (sometimes called 'modelling') and the various practices that are adopted or exhibited within a research context. These can be of substantial influence when considered within the context of highly structured organisations, such as the military.

Risks

In establishing the integrity of the methodology of narrative inquiry, the benefits of narrative cannot be viewed without due consideration of the *risks* involved (Figure 9.4). *Intersubjectivity* and *smoothing* are two important constraints and potential abuses of the narrative inquiry method, according to Connelly and Clandinin (1990). *Intersubjectivity* is the easy slipping into a commitment to the whole narrative plot and the researcher's role in it, without any appropriate reflection and analysis. *Smoothing* is the tendency to invoke a positive result regardless of the indications of the data. This can be approached through the use of 'critical others', as mentioned in Chapter 6.

As well as the risks that are intrinsic to the research approach, there are extrinsic risks, including those imposed by the constraints of the culture or the operational context of the study, sensitivities to times that discussions can be arranged with research participants and the 'state of mind' of participants (particularly following an especially demanding event).

Another constraint can be difficulty in gathering data in a way that does not interfere with the participants' conduct of work and other engagements and extremely tight scheduling of research sessions.

Results

Results need to be described in a way that will allow readers to revisit extracts of collected stories, to facilitate their own conclusions and understanding of the research data. We propose that a critical event approach to presenting data has substantial benefits for research using a narrative or storytelling approach. Details of the critical event approach, which categorises events as *critical, like* and *other* (Figure 9.5), are provided in Chapter 5. This approach overcomes the many difficulties associated with the management of large data sets. In essence it allows a 'mind filter' to influence the reporting; that is to say, the presented data consists of events recalled by research participants because of their impact and importance.

A framework example

The framework may 'come to life' by looking at how it fits a real-life example of narrative inquiry research. With this in mind, we use one of the research projects already referred to in earlier chapters to flesh out how the conceptual map of the framework reflects the actuality of a particular research project. We return to the project that included the story of the air traffic control trainee, first mentioned in Chapter 4. In applying the general to the specific, it is important to note that any

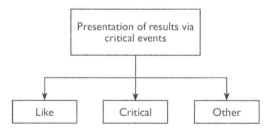

FIGURE 9.5   Outline of narrative inquiry results

particular research project will highlight some elements of the framework much more than others – this project certainly does.

In the previous section we presented the framework in a top-down manner. When beginning a research project, most time is spent at the level of detailed information gathering. Hence we have decided to build the overall picture of the research project by giving brief but specific details at the bottom level of the framework before summarising their relationships to the higher-level concepts that encapsulate those details. In other words, we use a bottom–up approach.

The project being described took place at different times and with different trainee groups in a training environment using high-fidelity simulators. Because this environment involved a mixture of teaching approaches, a mixture of data collection was required. A *survey* gathered biographical and educational background and enabled a sketch to be developed of the participants in the research project. *Interviews* were possible with both instructors and students, before and after simulator exercises, as was *observation* of the scheduled simulator tasks. In addition to observing the simulator task, a recording device was attached to the communications equipment of the simulator that enabled communications between instructor and student to be audio-recorded for later *transcription* and subsequent analysis. In addition, all *documentation* manuals for the complete training exercise, including classroom and simulator tasks, were made available to the researcher. The raw transcripts of the simulator tasks amounted to more than four volumes (more than 900 pages). Figure 9.6 summarises.

Establishing the validity and reliability of the research is a necessary part of any research report. In this project three elements of validity and reliability, as outlined

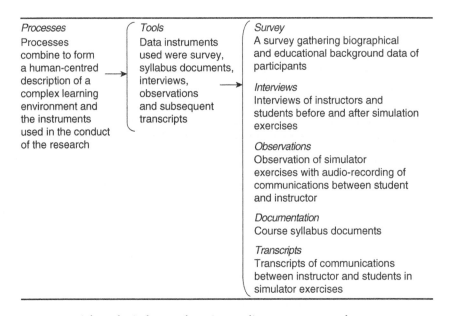

Processes	Tools	Survey
Processes combine to form a human-centred description of a complex learning environment and the instruments used in the conduct of the research	Data instruments used were survey, syllabus documents, interviews, observations and subsequent transcripts	A survey gathering biographical and educational background data of participants *Interviews* Interviews of instructors and students before and after simulation exercises *Observations* Observation of simulator exercises with audio-recording of communications between student and instructor *Documentation* Course syllabus documents *Transcripts* Transcripts of communications between instructor and students in simulator exercises

FIGURE 9.6 A hypothetical research project outline – processes: tools

in Chapter 6, stood out. At the lowest levels of the framework for this category, *access* to the codified data of all collected transcripts was ensured through indexing. Other data sources, including syllabus documentation, letters of permission to conduct the research in an operational setting specifying restrictions and constraints and examples of prototypes developed as an outcome of the research, ensured that a depth of probing could be conducted by any reader. The use of the *critical, like* and *other* events ensured a level of *verisimilitude*, as the detail and extent of transcripts would be difficult to replicate, except in the research context. *Transferability* was highlighted in this project through the construction of computer simulations that addressed specifically the confusions and complexities that arose during critical events. The use of critical, like and other events, by their very nature incorporating transferability of event, ensured a level of transferability between characters in the research as well as facilitating transfer to other contexts. Because this project involved the collection of a huge number of transcripts, it was important to have an *economical* approach to their analysis that would not compromise the validity of a human-centred approach to the research. A critical event approach provided that economy. *Honesty, authenticity* and *familiarity* were all present, but more in the background of the research. Figure 9.7 summarises.

Maps of the physical layout of buildings, offices, classrooms and simulators (tower and radar simulators combined with images of inside the simulator, diagrams detailing positions of instructional, 'pseudo' pilot and technology support staff) combine to *place* the research in its context. Other documentation, including the syllabus, details the *time* and sequencing of exercises and tasks required of the research participants. The *events* relevant to the research were identified through the trainee syllabus documentation (e.g. simulator sequences, course assessment and other training activities). Figure 9.8 summarises.

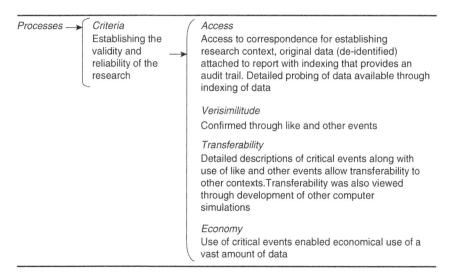

FIGURE 9.7   A hypothetical research project outline – processes: criteria

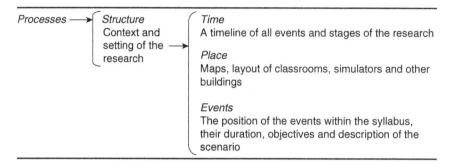

FIGURE 9.8 A hypothetical research project outline – processes: structure

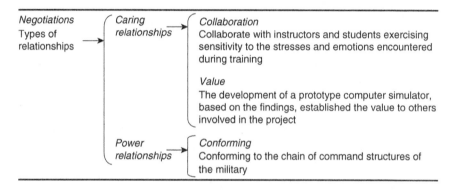

FIGURE 9.9 A hypothetical research project outline – negotiations

The research required the development of good relationships to enable effective capture of stories. The research was conducted in a military environment; power relationships were therefore fundamental to the research. *Conforming* to a chain of command had to be acknowledged and respected. Even though the research was conducted in a highly structured institutional environment, friendly, caring relationships were still essential. *Collaboration* with instructors facilitated discussion of complexities in the research context. Critical to this project was the need for the staff and trainees of the facility to see that there was *value* in the research. This was achieved through the development of computer-based simulations, which the instructors could use to further improve the learning and teaching of the air traffic control trainees under their instruction. *Community*, *collegiality*, *modelling* and *practice* were all present, but more in the background of the research. Figure 9.9 summarises.

Because the research was conducted in a military operational context, access to any of the facilities could be withdrawn at any time without any reason being given. There needed to be sensitivity to the demands placed on participants who were undergoing complex training. At times, this meant that the emotional needs of the trainees restricted access for interview or collection of data. These factors all created strong *external constraints* to the project. *Intersubjectivity* was a complex aspect of the project. It was partly avoided by collaboration with the education officer assigned to the training facility. On the other hand, because of the conditions of access imposed by the military, access by visiting experts and other critical friends was not permitted, which limited on-the-spot guidance by other experts. This, in part, was compensated for by careful and critical advice from a research supervisor. *Smoothing* was not an issue in this project. There were inherent problems with the training, and the military was open to having them investigated. Figure 9.10 summarises.

The processing and analysis of large amounts of collected data, particularly transcripts, was enabled by use of a critical event approach. With over four volumes of transcripts collected, the identification of critical, like and other events distilled the data into a manageable form, while at the same time ensuring that the focus of the research remained holistic and human centred. Over the extended period of the project, only a few detailed and critical events were highlighted, with a greater number of like and other events that supported and confirmed the critical events. Figure 9.11 summarises.

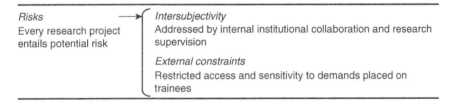

FIGURE 9.10 A hypothetical research project outline – risks

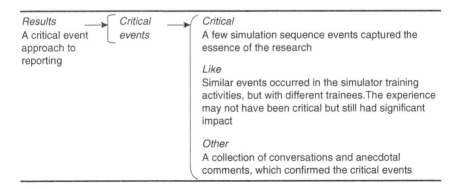

FIGURE 9.11 A hypothetical research project outline – results

A framework is a conceptual map. A map is nothing more than a representation of reality. Thus, it does not attempt to define reality but rather reflect reality, and it must always be open to adjustment and improvement. The authors of this book invite any researchers to review whether this framework is useful and apply it to their own investigations.

Positioning narrative inquiry

The use of human stories of experience as the basis of a research method is relatively recent when compared with other quantitative and qualitative research method frameworks. Two decades on since the 'narrative turn', and despite the fact that the awareness of narrative among researchers has grown and spread into a wide range of disciplines, it is still an emerging method. It is still being positioned within the domain of research methods. Although it is currently placed among qualitative research methods, we are of the view that, given its holistic nature and capacity for cross-cultural and cross-discipline research, narrative may be becoming established as a new category of research method based on human experience. It obviously differentiates itself not only from quantitative measurement approaches but also from many other qualitative methods. What makes it particularly suitable for research, both now and in the future, is its alignment with human experience in a complex (and constantly changing) world with needs that are not easily researched using traditional approaches. Table 9.1 outlines the way we perceive the positioning of narrative inquiry in the domain of research methods.

There are a number of traps or limitations that can be associated with the use of stories in research. Collection of data can easily lead to the collection of extensive amounts of data. Their transcription and subsequent analysis by current qualitative tools tend to encourage a narrowing view of the data and do not allow the story to evolve or identify those events that are critical. This can lead the researcher analyst into an endless *burrowing* process rather than a *broadening* approach. We believe that our proposed critical event narrative method is capable of avoiding this trap precisely by eliciting and focusing on the critical events in narratives of experience.

TABLE 9.1 Qualities of different research methods

Quantitative methods	Qualitative methods	Narrative inquiry
Measurable	Human element	Human experience
Descriptive/inferential statistics	Logical deduction	Convey/understand knowledge
Systematic	Content analysis	Critical events
Generalisable	Narrowing	Broadening
Large numbers	Small numbers	Small numbers

Narrative inquiry and future research needs

We are of the view that research using stories of experience offers useful insights into the problems and complexities faced by humankind. While we are mindful that there are undoubtedly many more, we outline four significant aspects of narrative inquiry that are of particular value in research: human centredness, learning and teaching, cross-discipline research and evaluation strategies.

Human-centred experience

In a changing world, there continues to be a rapid and exponential growth of knowledge. This creates new subcategories of knowledge and specialisations, which borrow methods and approaches from other closely related fields and, at the same time, approach spheres of knowledge of other disciplines. This growth of knowledge has created many new complexities for researchers and the need for a method that is holistic and not just discipline specific. It can be argued that human stories of experience provide a flexible and human-centred research approach to these issues.

Research in learning and teaching

This book is mostly concerned with new ways of conducting research. While education has long acknowledged the contributions of science and cognition to learning research, the educational research community has also intuitively accepted the reality that learning also involves 'something else', beyond the scientific and cognitive. This book, then, is one attempt to unpack that 'something else'.

The 'something else' in this book is reflected in human centredness and complexity – qualities of human life that we nominate as deep and overarching impulses and motivations for research.

We argue in this book that narrative brings to the forefront issues that are often masked by traditional, empirically based research methods. Narrative is sensitive to human factors and human understandings. Narrative presents a way of viewing the learning environment, framing the research methodology and presenting the findings. The stories generated in narrative reflect the complex, human-centred and dynamic nature of learning. Moreover, the findings of narrative inquiry may present an appropriate educational design platform for complex, dynamic and sophisticated technological learning environments, in highlighting learner issues that need to be addressed and possible strategies that can be used in supporting learning and performance.

Cross-discipline research

The ever-increasing boundaries of human knowledge are leading to the development of both new disciplines and new subdivisions within existing disciplines. Within research environments, particularly in areas that involve humans and some type of human experience, there is now increasing movement of methodological approaches. Stories have gained increasing stature outside the fields of literature and linguistics, becoming both a focus of research and a rich source of data in a range of disciplines.

For instance, the *Journal of Narrative and Life History* (1994) lists seven disciplines among the contributors of the journal. These are anthropology, education, folklore studies, linguistics, literary criticism, psychology and sociology. The 'narrative turn', particularly strong between the late 1980s and mid-1990s, is reflected in a growing number of narrative-focused publications in a range of disciplines such as history (e.g. White, 1981), anthropology and folklore (e.g. Behar, 1993), psychology (e.g. Bruner, 1986, 1987, 1990; Polkinghorne, 1988; Sarbin, 1986), sociology (e.g. Boje, 1991) and socio-linguistics (e.g. Labov, 1982; Polanyi, 1985).

Professions such as law, medicine, nursing and education have also discovered narrative. There are some notable publications in law (Amsterdam and Bruner, 2000; Bruner, 2002), in medicine (Hunter, 1991; Greenhalgh and Hurwitz, 1999) in nursing (Diekelmann, 2001; Ironside, 2003) and in education (Clandinin and Connelly, 1995, 2000; McEwan and Egan, 1995; Conle, 2000).

With the increasing complexity of human existence and the interrelatedness of aspects of knowledge that form our understanding, future research will need to be able to demonstrate a capacity to comfortably cross traditional discipline borders.

Narrative as an evaluation approach

Some authors (e.g. Polanyi, 1985; Linde, 1993) pointed out evaluation as a particularly valuable component of narrative. This might be attributed to the strong reflective component inherent in storytelling of human experience. Evaluation is ultimately concerned with identifying those features that made significant impact on a participant. We know that the mind filters the experiences we engage in every day and retains those that are most significant and changing. This is closely related to the notion of critical events outlined in this book. The value of this reflective process gives credibility to evaluation, while at the same time ensuring that we do not become too engaged in the minutiae of an event and miss the important impacts.

We are increasingly affected by an era of measurement and accountability. Our professional lives have seen an increase in performance-based approaches. In the case of higher education in Australia and other particularly Anglophone countries, measurement is directly linked to the funding of institutions provided by the governments. Based on the principles of accountability of public finances and 'quality' of higher education, evaluation is mandatory for institutions, if they wish to gain access to funding. It is evident that, with increasingly large stakes at hand, appropriate evaluation and measurement instruments are needed, particularly in areas of complex human endeavour. Human stories of experience would seem then to have much to offer to this measurement approach.

Either acting as a validation of more traditional instruments of evaluation or ensuring that key issues are identified, the use of storytelling in this environment is still in its early development. It offers much to the interested researcher. Perhaps its most obvious virtue to those engaged in evaluation is that storytelling is also perfectly compatible with, and can function as a validating instrument for, other qualitative and quantitative measures.

Conclusion

The significance of narrative inquiry lies in its exploration of new ways of viewing and conducting research that address human performance and experience in a variety of environments. In this book we have argued for the potential of collaboration between a wide range of research contexts and storytelling, have described features of a particular narrative inquiry approach applicable to a broad range of disciplines, have outlined in detail how to go about using this approach and have also given an example of research which utilized this method. We confirm narrative as an appropriate contemporary approach for research in complex, dynamic and high-performance environments and, in particular, for the study of human centredness and complexity.

BIBLIOGRAPHY

Adler, H.M. (1997) 'The history of the present illness as treatment: Who's listening, and why does it matter?' *Journal of the Board of Family Physicians*, 10: 28–35.

Agar, M., and Hobbs, J.R. (1982) 'Interpreting discourse: Coherence and the analysis of ethnographic interviews', *Discourse Processes*, 5: 1–32.

Akhtar, M., and Humphries, S. (2001) *The Fifties and Sixties: A Lifestyle Revolution*, London: Box Tree.

Amsterdam, A.G., and Bruner, J.S. (2000) *Minding the Law*, Cambridge, MA: Harvard University Press.

Anderson, D., and Johnson, R. (2006) *Ideas of Leadership Underpinning Proposals for the Carrick Institute: A Review of Proposals for the Leadership for Excellence in Teaching and Learning Program* (Occasional paper), available at: www.altc.edu.au/system/files/documents/grants_leadership_occasionalpaper_andersonandjohnson_nov06.pdf (accessed March 2013).

Angell, R. (1945) 'A critical review of the development of the personal document method in sociology 1920–1940', in L. Gottschalk, C. Kluckhohn, and R. Angell (eds.) *The Use of Personal Documents in History, Anthropology and Sociology*, New York: Social Science Research Council.

Angus, M. (1995) 'Writing about teaching', *25th Annual National Conference of the AARE*, Hobart, TAS, AARE, November, online, available at: www.aare.edu.au/ (accessed 06 June 2006).

Ball, S., and Goodson, I. (eds.) (1985) *Teachers' Lives and Careers*, London: Falmer Press.

Banathy, B. (1996) 'Systems inquiry and its application in education', in D. Jonassen (ed.) *Handbook of Research in Educational Communications and Technology*, New York: Simon and Schuster Macmillan.

Barnett, R. (1992) *Improving Higher Education: Total Quality Care*, Buckingham, UK: SRHE/Open University Press.

Barrett, M.S., and Stauffer, S.L. (eds.) (2009) *Narrative Inquiry in Music Education: Troubling Certainty*, Dordrecht, The Netherlands: Springer.

Beaty, D. (1995) *The Naked Pilot*, Shrewsbury, UK: Airlife Publishing.

Becher, T. (1989) *Academic Tribes and Territories: Intellectual Enquiry and the Cultures of the Disciplines*, Milton Keynes, UK: Society for Research into Higher Education and the Open University Press.

Becker, H.S. (1966) 'Introduction', in C. Shaw (ed.) *The Jack-Roller*, Chicago: University of Chicago Press.

Behar, R. (1993) *Translated Woman: Crossing the Border with Esperanza's Story*, Boston: Beacon.

Bell, J.S. (ed.) (1997) 'Teacher research in second and foreign language education' [special issue], *Canadian Modern Language Review*, 54(1).

Bell, J.S. (2002) 'Narrative inquiry: More than just telling stories', *TESOL Quarterly*, 36: 207–213.

Bell, M. (2004) 'Internationalising the higher education curriculum: Do academics agree?' *Proceedings of the 27th Higher Education Research & Development Society of Australasia (HERDSA) Conference*, Miri, Sarawak.

Bennett, D.C. (2001) 'Assessing quality in higher education', *Liberal Education*, 87(2), online, available at: www.aacu.org/publications-research/periodicals/assessing-quality-higher-education (accessed April 2019).

Berger, P.L., and Kellner, H. (1964) 'Marriage and the construction of reality', *Diogenes*, 46: 1–23.

Bertaux, D. (1981) *Biography and Society: The Life History Approach in the Social Sciences*, Beverly Hills, CA: Sage Publications.

Bishop, D.C., Crawford, K., Jenner, N., Liddle, N., Russell, E., and Woollard, M. (2012) 'Engaging students in quality processes', *Enhancing Learning in the Social Sciences*, 4(3): 1–6.

Bohl, N. (1995) 'Professionally administered critical incident debriefings for police officers', in M. Kurke (ed.) *Police Psychology into the 21st Century*, Washington, DC: APA Publishers.

Boje, D.M. (1991) 'The storytelling organization: A study of story performance in an office-supply firm', *Administrative Science Quarterly*, 36: 106–126.

Britton, J. (1970) *Language and Learning*, Harmondsworth, UK: Penguin.

Brown, A.L., and Palincsar, A.S. (1989) 'Guided, cooperative learning and individual knowledge acquisition', in L.B. Resnick (ed.) *Knowing, Learning and Instruction: Essays in Honour of Robert Glaser*, Hillsdale, NJ: Lawrence Erlbaum, pp. 393–451.

Brown, R. (2004) *Quality Assurance in Higher Education: The UK Experience Since 1992*, London: RoutledgeFalmer.

Bruner, J.S. (1986) *Actual Minds, Possible Worlds*, Cambridge, MA: Harvard University Press.

Bruner, J.S. (1987) 'Life as narrative', *Social Research*, 54: 11–32.

Bruner, J.S. (1990) *Acts of Meaning*, Cambridge, MA: Harvard University Press.

Bruner, J.S. (1991) 'The narrative construction of reality', *Critical Inquiry*, 18: 1–21.

Bruner, J.S. (1994) 'Life as narrative', in A.H. Dyson and C. Genishi (eds.) *The Need for Story: Cultural Diversity in Classroom and Community*, Urbana, IL: National Council of Teachers of English.

Bruner, J.S. (2002) *Making Stories: Law, Literature, Life*, New York: Farrar, Straus, and Giroux.

Byrne, M. (2001) 'Critical incident technique as a qualitative research method', *AORN Journal*, 74: 536–539.

Campbell, C., and van der Wende, M. (2000) *International Initiatives and Trends in Quality Assurance for European Higher Education: Exploratory Trend Report*, Helsinki: European Network of Quality Assurance Agencies.

Chambers *Combined Dictionary Thesaurus* (1997) 2nd edition, edited by M. Manser and M. Thomson, Edinburgh, UK: Chambers Harrap Publishers.

Carr, D. (1986) *Time, Narrative, and History*, Bloomington, IN: Indiana University Press.

Carson, D.A. (1996) *The Gagging of God*, Grand Rapids, MI: Zondervan.

Carter, K. (1993) 'The place of story in the study of teaching and teacher education', *Educational Researcher*, 22(1): 5–12.

Cartwright, J.M. (2007) 'The rhetoric and reality of "quality" in higher education: An investigation of staff perceptions of quality in post-1992 universities', *Quality Assurance in Education*, 15(3): 287–301.

Clandinin, D.J. (2006) 'Narrative inquiry: A methodology for studying lived experience', *Research Studies in Music Education*, 27: 44–54, Callaway Centre, online, available at: http://benjaminbolden.ca/wp-content/uploads/2015/09/2006-Clandinin-Narrative InquiryAMethodologyforStudyingLivedExperience.pdf (accessed January 2019).

Clandinin, D.J., and Caine, V. (2008) 'Narrative inquiry', in L.M. Given (ed.) *The Sage Encyclopedia of Qualitative Research Methods*, Thousand Oaks, CA: Sage Publications, pp. 542–545.

Clandinin, D.J., and Connelly, F.M. (1995) *Teachers' Professional Knowledge Landscapes*, New York: Teachers College Press.

Clandinin, D.J., and Connelly, F.M. (2000) *Narrative Inquiry: Experience and Story in Qualitative Research*, San Francisco: Jossey-Bass Publishers.

Cohen, L., Manion, L., and Morrison, K. (2000) *Research Methods in Education*, London: RoutledgeFalmer.

Conle, C. (2000) 'Narrative inquiry: Research tool and medium for professional development', *European Journal of Teacher Education*, 23: 49–63.

Connelly, F.M., and Clandinin, D.J. (1987) 'On narrative method, biography and narrative unities in the study of teaching', *Journal of Educational Thought*, 21: 130–139.

Connelly, F.M., and Clandinin, D.J. (1988) *Teachers as Curriculum Planners: Narratives of Experience*, New York: Teachers College Press.

Connelly, F.M., and Clandinin, D.J. (1990) 'Stories of experience and narrative inquiry', *Educational Researcher*, 19(5): 2–14.

Cortazzi, M. (1991) *Primary Teaching: How It Is – a Narrative Account*, London: David Fulton.

Daiute, C. (2014) *Narrative Inquiry: A Dynamic Approach*, Sage Publications.

Davidson, C.N. (1993) *36 Views of Mount Fuji: On Finding Myself in Japan*, New York: Dutton.

Denzin, N.K. (1970) *The Research Act*, Chicago: Aldine.

Dewey, P., and Duff, S. (2009) 'Reason for passion: Faculty views on internationalisation in higher education', *Higher Education*, 58(4): 491–504.

Diekelmann, N.L. (2001) 'Narrative pedagogy: Heideggerian hermeneutical analyses of lived experiences of students, teachers, and clinicians', *Advances in Nursing Science*, 23(3): 53–71.

Dollard, J. (1935) *Criteria for the Life History*, New Haven, CT: Yale University Press.

Dyson, A.H., and Genishi, C. (1994) *The Need for Story: Cultural Diversity in Classroom and Community*, Urbana, IL: National Council of Teachers of English.

Eisner, E.W. (1988) 'The primacy of experience and the politics of method', *Educational Researcher*, 17(5): 15–20.

Elbaz, F. (1990) 'Knowledge and discourse: The evolution of research on teacher thinking', in C. Day, M. Pope, and P. Denicolo (eds.) *Insights in Teachers' Thinking and Practice*, London: Falmer Press.

Elbaz, F. (1991) 'Research on teachers' knowledge: The evolution of discourse', *Journal of Curriculum Studies*, 23: 1–19.

Elliot, J. (2005) *Using Narrative in Social Research: Qualitative and Quantitative Approaches*, London: Sage Publications.

Erikson, E.H. (1956) 'The problem of identity', *Journal of American Psychoanalysis*, 4: 56–121.

European Educational Research Journal, special issue, Contemporary Methodological Diversity in European Higher Education Research, September (2013), 12(3): 301–415, online, available at: https://journals.sagepub.com/loi/eera?year=2013 (accessed January 2019).

Farran, D. (1990) 'Seeking Susan: Producing statistical information on young people's leisure', in L. Stanley (ed.) *Feminist Praxis*, London: Routledge.

Fay, J. (2000) 'A narrative approach to critical and sub-critical incident debriefings', published dissertation, American School of Professional Psychology, online, available at: www.narrativeapproaches.com (accessed 09 June 2006).

Flick, U. (1998) *An Introduction to Qualitative Research*, London: Sage Publications.

Fountain, J.E. (1999) 'A note on the critical incident technique and its utility as a tool of public management research', *Annual Meeting of the Association of Public Policy and Management*, Washington, DC, 4–6 November.

Fullan, M. (1991) *The Meaning of Educational Change*, New York: Teachers College Press.

Gann, E. (1961) *Fate Is the Hunter*, New York: Touchstone.

Gawande, A. (2005) 'The character of a doctor', *Focus: The Australian Doctor Magazine*, March: 28–30.

Ganzevoort, R. (2005) *Reading by the Lines: Proposal for a Narrative Analytical Technique in Empirical Theology*, online, available at: www.ruardganzevoort.nl (accessed 14 June 2006).

Geelan, D. (2003) *Weaving Narrative Nets to Capture Classrooms*, London: Kluwer Academic Publishers.

Geertz, C. (1973) *The Interpretation of Cultures*, New York: Basic Books.

Gertsen, M.C., and Soderberg, A-M. (2011) 'Intercultural collaboration stories: On narrative inquiry and analysis as tolls for research in international business', *Journal of International Business Studies*, 42(6): 787–804.

Glaser, B., and Strauss, A.L. (1967) *Discovery of Grounded Theory*, Chicago: Aldine.

Gough, N. (1991) 'An abominable snow job: Systems models and the Himalayan "eco-crisis" in VCE environmental studies', *Eingana*, 4: 24–26.

Gough, N. (1994) 'Research in fiction: Detective stories as analogues of educational inquiry', *Annual Conference of the Australian Association for Research in Education (AARE)*, Newcastle, NSW, November.

Gough, N. (1997) *Horizons, Images and Experiences: The Research Stories Collection*, Geelong, VIC: Deakin University.

Graham, R.J. (1992) 'Currere and reconceptualisation: The progress of the pilgrimage 1975–1990', *Journal of Curriculum Studies*, 24: 27–42.

Green, B., and Reid, J. (1995) 'Educational research, teacher education, and practical theory: Towards an account of poststructuralism and pedagogy', *25th Annual National Conference of the AARE*, Hobart, TAS, November, online, available at: www.aare. edu.au (accessed 06 June 2006).

Green, D. (1994) 'What is quality in higher education? Concepts, policy and practice', in D. Green (ed.) *What Is Quality in Higher Education?*, Buckingham: SRHE/Open University Press, pp. 3–20.

Green, W. (2017) 'Enabling narrative in the "unhomely" field of higher education research', in S. Trahar and W.M. Yu (eds.) *Using Narrative Inquiry for Educational Research in the Asia Pacific*, Routledge, pp. 14–29.

Green, W. and Mertova, P. (2009) *Internationalisation of Teaching and Learning at the University of Queensland: Perceptions and Practices*, Brisbane, Australia: University of Queensland.

Green, W., and Mertova, P. (2010) 'Listening to the gatekeepers: Faculty perspectives on developing curriculum for globally responsible citizenship', *Internationalisation of the Curriculum Conference 2010, Internationalisation of the Curriculum for Global Citizenship: Policies, Practices and Pitfalls,* June, Oxford, UK.

Green, W., and Mertova, P. (2011) 'Listening to the gatekeepers: Faculty perspectives on developing curriculum for globally responsible citizenship', in V. Clifford and C. Montgomery (eds.) *Internationalisation of the Curriculum for Global Citizenship: Policies, Practices and Pitfalls*, Oxford: Oxford Centre for Staff and Learning Development (OCSLD).

Green, W., and Mertova, P. (2014) 'Enthusiasts, fence-sitters and sceptics: A comparative study of faculty perspectives on study abroad in Australia and the Czech Republic', *Higher Education Research and Development (HERD)*, 33(4): 670–683.

Green, W., and Mertova, P. (2016) 'Transformalists and transactionists: Towards a comprehensive understanding of academics engagement with "internationalisation of the curriculum"', *Research in Comparative and International Education*, 11(3): 1–18.

Greenhalgh, T., and Hurwitz, B. (1999) 'Narrative based medicine: Why study narrative?' *British Medical Journal*, 318: 48–50.

Grumet, M.R. (1976) 'Existential and phenomenological foundations', in W.F. Pinar and M.R. Grumet (eds.) *Toward a Poor Curriculum*, Dubuque, IA: Kendall Hunt.

Grumet, M.R. (1981) 'Restitution and reconstruction of educational experience: An autobiographical method for curriculum theory', in L. Martin and L. Barton (eds.) *Rethinking Curriculum Studies: A Radical Approach*, London: Croom Helm.

Guba, E.G., and Lincoln, Y.S. (1981) *Effective Evaluation: Improving the Usefulness of Evaluation Results Through Responsive and Naturalistic Approaches*, San Francisco: Jossey-Bass.

Gudmundsdottir, S. (1995) 'The narrative nature of pedagogical content knowledge', in H. McEwan and K. Egan (eds.) *Narrative in Teaching, Learning and Research*, New York: Teachers College Press.

Hager, P. (2004) 'Conceptions of learning and understanding learning at work', *Studies in Continuing Education*, 26(1): 3–17.

Hanrahan, M., and Cooper, T. (1995) 'Aye, its delicious, but tha's no' how y' make porridge! Personal writing for learning in a science education PhD', *25th Annual National Conference of the AARE*, Hobart, TAS, November, online, available at: www.aare. edu.au/ (accessed 06 June 2006).

Harding, S. (1986) *The Science Question in Feminism*, Ithaca, NY: Cornell University Press.

Hardy, B. (1977) 'Narrative as a primary act of mind', in M. Meek, A. Warlow, and G. Barton (eds.) *The Cool Web*, London: Bodley Head.

Harvey, H., and Green, D. (1993) 'Defining quality', *Assessment and Evaluation in Higher Education*, 18(1): 9–34.

Harvey, L. (1998) 'An assessment of past and current approaches to quality in higher education', *Australian Journal of Education*, 42(3): 237–255.

Harvey, L. (2004) 'Let's stop this shameful elitism 4', *Times Higher Education Supplement*, 15 October.

Harvey, L. (2005) 'A history and critique of quality evaluation in the UK', *Quality Assurance in Education*, 13(4): 263–276.

Hauerwas, S., and Burren, D. (1989) 'From system to story', in S. Hauerwas and L.G. Jones (eds.) *Why Narrative: Readings in Narrative Theology*, Grand Rapids, MI: Eerdmans Publishing.

Hauerwas, S., and Jones, L.G. (1989) *Why Narrative: Readings in Narrative Theology*, Grand Rapids, MI: Eerdmans Publishing.

Heath, S.B. (1983) *Ways with Words: Language, Life, and Work in Communities and Classrooms*, New York: Cambridge University Press.

Hellman, A.P. (2005) 'Narrative and illness: The death of a doctor's friend', *Medical Journal of Australia*, 182: 9–11.

Henson, L. (1992) 'The Momina theme of life: Developed biblically, theologically and contextually', unpublished PhD thesis, Fuller Theological Seminary, Los Angeles.

Herman, D. (1999) *Narratologies: New Perspectives on Narrative Analysis*, Columbus, OH: Ohio State University Press.

Hewitt, R. (2019) 'Measuring well-being in higher education', *HEPI Policy Note 13*, online, available at: www.hepi.ac.uk/2019/05/09/measuring-well-being-in-higher-education/ (accessed 16 May 2019).

Hlynka, D., and Belland, J.C. (1991) *Paradigms Regained: The Uses of Illuminative, Semiotic, and Post-Modern Criticism as Modes of Inquiry in Educational Technology*, Englewood Cliffs, NJ: Educational Technology Publications.

Huberman, M. (1995) 'Working with life-history narratives', in H. McEwan and K. Egan (eds.) *Narrative in Teaching, Learning and Research*, New York: Teachers College Press.

Hunter, K. (1991) *Doctors' Stories*, Princeton, NJ: Princeton University Press.

Ironside, P.M. (2003) 'New pedagogies for teaching thinking: The lived experiences of students and teachers enacting narrative pedagogy', *Journal of Nursing Education*, 42: 509–516.

Jack, A. (2019) 'UK Universities face their toughest test', *Financial Times*, 5 February, online, available at: https://www.ft.com/content/46582248-133a-11e9-a581-4ff78404524e (accessed September 2019).

Jalongo, M.R., and Isenberg, J.P. (1995) *Teachers' Stories: From Personal Narrative to Professional Insight*, San Francisco: Jossey-Bass Publishers.

Jonassen, D.H. (1997) *Mind Tools for Schools*, New York: Macmillan.

Jones, S. (2003) 'Measuring the quality of higher education: Linking teaching quality measures at the delivery level to administrative measures at the university level', *Quality in Higher Education*, 9(3): 223–229.

Josselson, R. (1996) *Ethics and Process in the Narrative Study of Lives*, Thousand Oaks, CA: Sage Publications.

Josselson, R., and Lieblich, A. (1993) *The Narrative Study of Lives*, Newbury Park, CA: Sage Publications.

Journal of Narrative and Life History, 4 (1994), online, available at: https://benjamins.com/catalog/jnlh (accessed September 2019).

Juntrasook, A. (2017) 'A journey in the land of the long white cloud: A Thai academic doing narrative inquiry in Aotearoa New Zealand', in S. Trahar and W.M. Yu (eds.) *Using Narrative Inquiry for Educational Research in the Asia Pacific*, Routledge, pp. 1–14.

Kim, J-H. (2016) *Understanding Narrative Inquiry*, Sage Publications.

Knight, J. (1999) 'Internationalisation of Higher Education', in H. DeWit & J. Knight (eds.) *Quality and Internationalisation in Higher Education*, Paris: Organisation for Economic Cooperation and Development, pp. 13–28.

Knight, J. (2004) 'Internationalization remodeled: Definition, approaches and rationales', *Journal of Studies in International Education*, 8(1): 5–31.

Kraft, C.H. (1979) *Christianity in Culture*, Maryknoll, NY: Orbis Books.

Kuhns, R. (1974) *Structures of Experience*, New York: Harper and Row.

Labov, W. (1982) *Analysing Discourse: Text and Talk*, Washington, DC: Georgetown University Press.

Lather, P. (1993) 'Fertile obsession: Validity after poststructuralism', *The Sociological Quarterly*, 34: 673–693.

Laub, J.H., and Sampson, R.J. (1998) 'Integrating quantitative and qualitative data', in J.Z. Giele and G.H. Elder (eds.) *Methods of Life Course Research: Qualitative and Quantitative Approaches*, Thousand Oaks, CA: Sage Publications.

Lieblich, A., Tuval-Mashiach, R., and Zilber, T. (1998) *Narrative Research: Reading, Analysis and Interpretation*, Thousand Oaks, CA: Sage Publications.

Lincoln, Y.S., and Guba, E.G. (1985) *Naturalistic Inquiry*, Beverly Hills, CA: Sage Publications.

Linde, C. (1993) *Life Stories: The Creation of Coherence*, Oxford, UK: Oxford University Press.

Lloyd, D. (2018) 'The future of higher education', *TEQSA 2018 Conference*, 28–30 November, available at: www.teqsa.gov.au/teqsa-conference-2018 (accessed April 2019).

Lomas, L. (2000) 'Senior staff member perception of organisational culture and quality in higher education institutions in England', unpublished PhD thesis, University of Kent, UK.

Lomas, L. (2004) 'Embedding quality: The challenges for higher education', *Quality Assurance in Education*, 12(4): 157–165.

Lomas, L. (2007) 'Are students customers? Perceptions of academic staff', *Quality in Higher Education*, 13(1): 31–44.

MacIntyre, A. (1981) *After Virtue*, Notre Dame, IN: University of Notre Dame Press.

MacIntyre, A. (1988) *Whose Justice? Which Rationality?* Notre Dame, IN: University of Notre Dame Press.

Marginson, S. (2007) 'Global position and position-taking: The case of Australia', *Journal of Studies in International Education*, 11(1): 5–32.

Markham, B. (1994) *The Illustrated West with the Night*, New York: Welcome Enterprises.

Mathias, H. (2004) 'The missing "E" factor in "QA"', *Learning Matters*, Newsletter No 14, April, Institute of Education, University of London: 1–2.

May, V.V., Luxon, T.H., Weaver, K., Esselstein, R., and Char, C. (2008) 'Development of case stories by interviewing students about their critical moments in science, math, and engineering classes', *Numeracy*, 1(1).

McEwan, H., and Egan, K. (1995) *Narrative in Teaching, Learning and Research*, New York: Teachers College Press.

Measor, L. (1985) 'Critical incidents in the classroom: Identities, choices and careers', in S. Ball and I. Goodson (eds.) *Teachers' Lives and Careers*, London: Falmer Press.

Merrill, D. (1996) *Reclaiming the Discipline of Instructional Design*, online, available at: http://itech1.coe.uga.edu/itforum (accessed 15 June 2006).

Mertova, P. (2008) 'Quality in higher education: Stories of English and Czech academics and higher education leaders', unpublished PhD thesis, Monash University, Melbourne, Australia.

Miles, M.B., and Huberman, A.M. (1994) *Qualitative Data Analysis: An Expanded Source-Book*, Thousand Oaks, CA: Sage Publications.

Ministry of Education, Youth and Sports of the Czech Republic (2001a) *Strategie terciarni sfery vzdelavani (Strategic Development of the Tertiary Education)*.

Ministry of Education, Youth and Sports of the Czech Republic (2001b) *National Programme for the Development of Education in the Czech Republic*, White Paper, pp. 75–76, online, available at: http://aplikace.msmt.cz/pdf/whitepaper.pdf (accessed March 2013).

Mishler, E.G. (1986) *Research Interviewing: Context and Narrative*, Cambridge, MA: Harvard University Press.

Mishler, E.G. (1990) 'Validation in inquiry-guided research: The role of exemplars in narrative studies', *Harvard Educational Review*, 60: 414–442.

Mitchell, W.J.T. (ed.) (1981) *On Narrative*, Chicago: Chicago University Press.

Morgan, M. (2019) *Improving the Student Experience in Higher Education*, website, available at: www.improvingthestudentexperience.com/why-improve-student-experience/ (accessed April 2019).

Morley, L. (1997) 'Change and equity in higher education', *British Journal of Sociology of Education*, 18(2): 231–242.

Nadler, L. (1982) *Designing Training Programs: The Critical Events Model*, Reading, MA: Addison–Wesley Publishing Company.

Naidu, S., and Cunnigton, D. (2004) 'Showcasing faculty experiences with technology enhanced teaching and learning', *AACE Journal*, 12: 141–154.

Narrative *Inquiry Journal*, John Benjamins Publishing Company, online, available at: www.ingentaconnect.com/content/jbp/nari (accessed January 2019).

Neisser, U., and Fivush, R. (1994) *The Remembering Self*, Cambridge, UK: Cambridge University Press.

Newton, J. (2001) 'Views from below: Academics coping with quality', Keynote Presentation at 6th QHE Seminar: End of Quality? 25–26 May, EAIR/SRHE, Birmingham, UK.

Ommundsen, W. (1993) *Metafictions? Reflexivity in Contemporary Texts*, Melbourne, VIC: Melbourne University Press.

Patton, M.Q. (2002) *Qualitative Research and Evaluation Methods*, Thousand Oaks, CA: Sage Publications.

Pearce, L.D. (2002) 'Integrating survey and ethnographic methods for systematic anomalous case analysis', *Sociological Methodology*, 32: 103–132.

Pinar, W.F. (1975a) 'Currere: Towards reconceptualisation', in W.F. Pinar (ed.) *Curriculum Theorizing: The Reconceptualists*, Berkely, CA: McCutchan.

Pinar, W.F. (1975b) 'The analysis of educational experience', in W.F. Pinar (ed.) *Curriculum Theorizing: The Reconceptualists*, Berkely, CA: McCutchan.

Pinar, W.F. (1975c) 'Search for a method', in W.F. Pinar (ed.) *Curriculum Theorizing: The Reconceptualists*, Berkely, CA: McCutchan.

Polanyi, L. (1985) *Telling the American Story*, Norwood, NJ: Ablex.

Polanyi, M. (1964) *The Educated Imagination*, Bloomington, IN: Indiana University Press.

Polkinghorne, D.E. (1988) *Narrative Knowing and the Human Sciences*, Albany, NY: State University of New York Press.

Reeves, T. (1996) 'A hopefully humble paradigm review', *ITFORUMDigest*, 21 February, online, available at: http://itech1.coe.uga.edu/itforum (accessed 15 June 2006).

'Reflection on narrative by Dr Sue McNamara' (2005) unpublished, interview held in October.

'Reflection on narrative by Dr Les Henson' (2006) unpublished, Tabor, VIC, written in February.

'Reflective stories of course participants in a Graduate Certificate in Law Teaching in 2003' (2003) unpublished, Faculty of Law, Monash University, VIC.

Reighart, P.A., and Loadman, W.E. (1984) 'Content analysis of student critical events reported in the professional introduction courses', report, Ohio State University.

Richardson, V. (ed.) (2001) *Handbook of Research on Teaching*, Washington, DC: American Educational Research Association.

Riessman, C.K. (1993) *Narrative Analysis*, Newbury Park, CA: Sage Publications.

Rimmon-Kenan, S. (1983) *Narrative Fiction: Contemporary Poetics*, London: Methuen.

Rosen, H. (1985) *Stories and Meaning*, Sheffield: National Association for the Teaching of English.

Ryan, T. (2015) 'Quality assurance in higher education: A review of literature', *Higher Learning Research Communications*, 5(4), online, https://doi.org/10.18870/hlrc.v5i4.257 (accessed April 2019).

Sacks, O. (1998) *The Man Who Mistook His Wife for a Hat and Other Clinical Tales*, New York: Touchstone.

Saint-Exupery, A. de (1943) *Night Flight*, translated by S. Gilbert, Melbourne, VIC: Lothian.

Saint-Exupery, A. de (1945) *The Little Prince*, translated by K. Woods, London: William Heinemann.

Sanderson, G. (2008) 'A foundation for the internationalization of the academic self in higher education', *Journal of Studies in International Education*, 12(3): 276–307.

Sarbin, T.R. (1986) *Narrative Psychology: The Storied Nature of Human Conduct*, New York: Praeger.

Sartre, J-P. (1964) *Words*, New York: Braziller.

Schoenfeld, A.H. (1999) 'Looking toward the 21st century: Challenges of educational theory and practice', *Educational Researcher*, 28(7): 4–14.

Schon, D. (1983) *The Reflective Practitioner: How Professionals Think in Action*, New York: Basic Books.

Schwartz, S. (2013) *Oliver Smithies Lecture on 'Knowledge Without Wisdom'*, Oxford: Balliol College, 28 February.

Seidman, I. (1998) *Interviewing as Qualitative Research*, New York: Teachers College Press.

Shaw, C.R. (1930) *The Jack-Roller*, Chicago: University of Chicago Press.

Shaw, C.R. (1931) *The Natural History of a Delinquency Career*, Chicago: Chicago University Press.

Shaw, C.R. *et al.* (1938) *Brothers in Crime*, Chicago: Chicago University Press.

Shields, C.M., Bishop, R., and Mazawi, A.E. (2005) *Pathologizing Practices: The Impact of Deficit Thinking on Education*, New York: Peter Lang.

Shulman, L. (1987) 'Knowledge and teaching foundations of the new reform', *Harvard Educational Review*, 57: 1–22.

Shute, V.J., and Gawlick-Grendell, L.A. (1992) *If Practice Makes Perfect, What Does Less Practice Make?* Brooks AFB, TX: Armstrong Lab, Human Resources Directorate.

Sikes, P. *et al.* (1985) *Teacher Careers: Crises and Continuities*, Lewes, UK: FalmerPress.

Silverman, D. (2000) *Doing Qualitative Research: A Practical Handbook*, London: Sage Publications.

Social Research Centre (2019) *Quality Indicators in Learning and Teaching (QILT)*. Website, available at: www.qilt.edu.au/about-this-site/student-experience/ (accessed April 2019).

Sparkes, A.C. (1988) 'Strands of commitment within the process of teacher initiated innovation', *Educational Review*, 40: 301–317.

Stake, R. *et al.* (1978) *Case Studies in Science Education*, Center for Instructional Research and Curriculum Evaluation, University of Illinois, Washington, DC: US Government Printing Office.

Stoddart, J. (2004) 'Foreword', in R. Brown (ed.) *Quality Assurance in Higher Education: The UK Experience Since 1992*, London, UK: RoutledgeFalmer, pp. x–xiii.

'Stories of academics in higher education quality' (2006) A collection of stories in higher education, unpublished, Monash University, VIC.

'Stories of educational developers in psychiatry' (2006) A collection of stories of educational developers in psychiatry, unpublished, Monash University, VIC.

'Stories of professional practice' (2005) A collection of stories by educational developers, law teachers and other professionals, unpublished, Monash University, VIC.

Strauss, A.L. (1959) *Mirrors and Masks: The Search for Identity*, Glencoe, IL: Free Press.

Strauss, A.L., and Corbin, J. (1990) *Basics of Qualitative Research: Grounded Theory Procedures and Techniques*, Newbury Park, CA: Sage Publications.

Strauss, A.L., and Corbin, J. (1998) *Basics of Qualitative Research: Grounded Theory Procedures and Techniques*, 2nd edition, Thousand Oaks, CA: Sage Publications.

Theobald, R. (1998) *Robert Theobald and the Healing Century*, ABC Radio National, Australian Broadcasting Commission, broadcast on 5 April, online, available at: www.abc.net.au (accessed 15 June 2006).

Thomas, W.I. (1923) *The Unadjusted Girl*, Boston: Little, Brown and Co.

Thomas, W.I., and Znaniecki, F. (1958) *The Polish Peasant in Europe and America*, New York: Dover.

Thompson, P. (2004) 'Researching family and social mobility with two eyes: Some experiences of the interaction between qualitative and quantitative data', *International Journal of Social Research Methodology*, 7: 237–257.

Todd, S. (2018) 'Foreword', *Irish Educational Studies*, 37(2), online, available at: www.tandfonline.com/toc/ries20/37/2?nav=tocList (accessed January 2019).

Toffler, A. (1998) *Life Matters*, ABC Radio National, Australian Broadcasting Commission, broadcast on 5 March, online, available at: www.abc.net.au (accessed 14 July 2006).

Trahar, S. (2010) *Developing Cultural Capability in International Higher Education: A Narrative Inquiry*, Routledge.

Trahar, S. (ed.) (2013) *Contextualising Narrative Inquiry: Developing Methodological Approaches for Local Contexts*, Routledge.

Trahar, S., and Yu, W.M. (eds.) (2017a) *Using Narrative Inquiry for Educational Research in the Asia Pacific*, Routledge.

Trahar, S., and Yu, W.M. (2017b) 'Preface', in S. Trahar and W.M. Yu (eds.) *Using Narrative Inquiry for Educational Research in the Asia Pacific*, Routledge, pp. xii–xxviii.

Van Damme, D. (2001) 'Quality issues in the internationalisation of higher education', *Higher Education*, 41: 415–441.

Van der Wende, M.C., and Westerheijden, D.F. (2001) 'International aspects of quality assurance with a special focus on European higher education', *Quality in Higher Education*, 7(3): 233–245.

Van de Walle, R. (2018) 'We are transforming our university into a place where talent once again feels valued and nurtured', online, available at: www.ugent.be/en/news-events/ghent-university-talent-rat-race-transformation-career-evaluation-model.htm (accessed March 2019).

Walker, R. *et al.* (1976) *Innovation, the School and the Teacher (1), Open University Course E203 Unit 27*, Milton Keynes, UK: Open University Press.

Wang, C.C., and Geale, S.K. (2015) 'The power of story: Narrative inquiry as a methodology in nursing research', *International Journal of Nursing Sciences*, 2(2): 195–198.

Watson, D. (1995) 'Quality assessment and "self-regulation": The English experience, 1992–94', *Higher Education Quarterly*, 49(4): 326–340.

Webster, L.L. (1998) 'A story of instructional research and simulation in aviation (air traffic control)', unpublished doctoral thesis, Monash University, VIC.

Webster, L.L., and Mertova, P. (2007) *Using Narrative Inquiry as a Research Method: An Introduction to Using Critical Event Narrative Analysis in Research on Learning and Teaching*, London, UK, Routledge.

Welty, E. (1979) *The Eye of the Story: Selected Essays and Reviews*, New York: Vintage Books.

Westerheijden, D.F. *et al.* (eds.) (1994) *Changing Contexts of Quality Assessment: Recent Trends in West European Higher Education*, Utrecht, Netherlands: Uitgeverij Lemma B.V.

White, H. (1981) 'The value in the representation of reality', in W.J.T. Mitchell (ed.) *On Narrative*, Chicago: Chicago University Press.

Wilger, A. (1997) *Quality Assurance in Higher Education: A Literature Review*, National Center for Postsecondary Improvement, School of Education, Stanford University, online, available at: https://web.stanford.edu/group/ncpi/documents/pdfs/6-03b_qualityassurance.pdf (accessed August 2019).

Winch, C. (1998) *The Philosophy of Human Learning*. Routledge International Studies in the Philosophy of Education, London and New York: Routledge.

Woods, P. (1993a) *Critical Events in Teaching and Learning*, Basingstoke, UK: Falmer Press.

Woods, P. (1993b) 'Critical events in education', *British Journal of Sociology of Education*, 14: 355–371.

Yeaman, A.R.J. (1996) 'Postmodern and poststructural theory version 1.0', in D.H. Jonassen (ed.) *Handbook of Research for Educational Communications and Technology*, New York: Simon & Schuster Macmillan.

Yoder-Wise, P.S., and Kowalski, K. (2003) 'The power of storytelling', *Nursing Outlook*, 51: 37–42.

INDEX

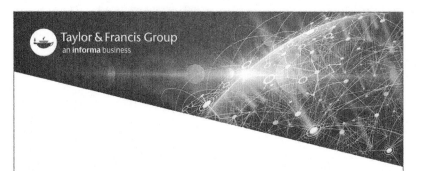